A BRITISH LOVE STORY

Joyful Professor's Journey to London & The UK

"This love story begins in Augsburg Germany, where Arthur as a Second Lieutenant, first meets his lovely future British wife - and it was "Love at First Sight"

He also fell in love with Great Britain when they first visited together soon thereafter and before their marriage later when Arthur was then a Captain and Company Commander!

Then years later, - As an Attorney and Law Professor:

Loving British Living, and exploring with his lovely new Dutch wife and darling daughters!

Arthur De La Loza, Esq., J.D., LL.M.

Table of Contents

Dedication

"With thanks to God, my very hardworking parents, teachers, and lovely family members and friends who made me who I am today: from a poor shoeshine boy - selling newspapers on the street corner to a proud Global Attorney, International Law Professor, Banker, and Travel Study Grad and undergraduate Professor of US-EU Law!"

My beautiful darling parents!

Love you in heaven now, Rest in Peace!

Book Outline

"An Officer and Gentleman" - first falling in love with his British wife - then years later, His lovely new Dutch wife and darling daughters -love Great Britain, and the British - as a thankful professor teaching in London and living and loving the countryside, arts and culture: exploring galleries, theaters, music venues, festivals, and cultural events in the city."

Yes, I do speak English! And yes, falling in love immediately sounds intriguing!

"It was a lovely but busy early evening on the street called Koenigsplatz in Augsburg, Germany, and Arthur had just been deployed there as a Second Lieutenant after completing his U.S. Army OCS Training!"

Then, at 6 PM, in Augsburg, Bavaria, Germany, when the young Second Lieutenant, Arthur, having just been deployed, walks up to a beautiful lady waiting for a bus in the downtown area and says, "Do you speak English?" Falling in love with her beautiful blue eyes, she replies with a gorgeous English accent, "I am English." This would be the beginning of all the loveliest British chapters in Arthur's life. He then asked, "Do you know where The Big Apple bar or pub is?" She said, "Yes, it's just down the street, on the left-hand side."

Arthur had just arrived in Bavaria, having lived the most fun years of his life in Hollywood on the corner of Melrose and Vine, attending and enjoying wonderful places like the Whisky a Go Go, and PJs where he danced the night away with lovely and exciting ladies. This was his "Once Upon a Time in Hollywood." He would soon meet up with this lovely English lady, ask her to dance, and love her very modest dance moves - compared to the then incredible dancing that he experienced in Hollywood. "An Officer and a Gentleman" was something they would watch years later, with tears, still caring deeply thereafter.

Lyrics Song by Jennifer Warnes and Joe Cocker, "Up Where We Belong:"

"Who knows what tomorrow brings

In a world few hearts survive

All I know is the way I feel when it's real,

I keep it alive

The road is long

There are mountains in our way

But we climb a step every day

Love lift us up where we belong

Where the eagles cry,

On a mountain high

Love lift us up where we belong

Far from the world below

Up where the clear winds blow"

Source: Lyric Find

Songwriters: Buffy Saint-Marie/Jack Nitzsche/ Will Jennings

"Up Where We Belong" lyrics @ Sony/ATV Music Publishing LLC

Having been together for some time, they reminisced with tears in their eyes about the fond memories of their time in Germany. He was in the service, and she was working at one of the military kasernes in the supermarket while studying French.

Top Teaching and Military Examples in Arthur's Life!

Arthur joined the military in 1966 for four years, until 1970. He attended Aberdeen, Maryland Proving Grounds OCS from 1966 to 1967. With much gratitude and thanks to his sister Natalie's husband, Ernie, who was a member of ROTC and wore his uniform with much pride, setting a great example for young people in our family. And, of course, my wonderful Dad, who was a WWII wounded warrior and earned the Purple Heart, as well as his brothers who served with honor as well.

Life in the UK was in 2003 and 2004. Arthur then lived in the Swiss Alps near Lake Geneva. He returned to lovely Britain in 2008, enjoying activities such as running and bike rides around Benbow Pond, golfing at Cowdray Golf, and watching polo at Cowdray Estate. He also explored the Cowdray Estate and Ruins, as well as the Midhurst East Off-Road Cycle Routes. He particularly loved Montreux, Switzerland, during his time there.

Arthur's other sister, Irene, visited Europe with her very talented husband, a Licensed Land Surveyor named Bill. They met in Montreux, Switzerland, near Arthur's home in the Alps, for the Jazz Festival. Incidentally, Arthur's brother-in-law also visited Arthur's home in Newport Beach and surveyed the lot lines, adding 600 sq ft to the 10,000 sq ft lot. Arthur expressed his gratitude to Bill and his sister, saying, "Thank you, Bill. Love you guys!"

The Montreux Jazz Festival, with nearly 250,000 spectators each year, offers a breathtaking setting and concerts with renowned acoustics. Established in 1967, it has become a must-attend event for music lovers worldwide. Featuring performances from the likes of Miles Davis, Ray Charles, David Bowie, and Prince, the festival showcases various music styles. The intimate setting of the Montreux Jazz Festival provides an ideal platform for both musicians and the public. For more information, you can visit the festival's website at http://www.montreuxjazzfestival.com.

My Wonderfully Talented and Brilliant Sisters.

Teachers in Life

Proud Pop!

Lovely Daughter and Mommy of my Grandson!

Proud Brother in Arms!

A thankful Professor's London teaching-and Loving -his family's time enjoying all of Britain's lovely people, Arts and Culture: and his opportunity for Exploring the lovely countryside -where he and his family Lived-As well as the Galleries, Theaters, Music Venues, Festivals, and Cultural Events in the City - with much gratitude and joy!

"You can't describe it, words don't do it justice. You just have to come and experience it."

Quincy Jones, Montreux Jazz Festival.

Arthur met this lovely British lady after OCS in 1967 in Germany. They then lived together in Kansas in 1968, where she was a student with a visa as a British national. Arthur was then deployed to Grafenwoehr, Germany, in 1968 when Czechoslovakia was invaded by the Warsaw Pact nations.

The 7th Army Training Command (7th ATC), headquartered at Tower Barracks in Grafenwoehr, Germany, resources the training readiness for all of U.S. Army Europe and Africa's (USAREUR-AF) assigned and allocated forces, along with Allied and partner nations upon request, throughout the U.S. European Command area of operations with the following organizations:

While in the US, he was sent to and went to Camp La Crosse, Wisconsin. Then, his beautiful British girlfriend came to visit him on the bus from Kansas.

Almost lost his life! He took her back to the bus station in his car, a Mercedes 230 SL that he bought while he was in Germany. After he left her off at the bus station, he was returning to Post on an icy road and tried to avoid hitting a deer. Losing control of his car, it slid off the road, came in contact with the dirt sideways, and rolled over, throwing him out of the car. At that point, the vehicle continued to roll towards him and landed on his back, burning through his clothing with the heated exhaust pipes. He was stuck under the car and decided to crawl out, barely making it to the side of the road when a vehicle came by. The driver asked if he needed any help, and he said, "Yes, please call the ambulance." The man said, "I would help you, but I'm a paraplegic, bad news." The good news was that he was also a radio man for the local highway patrol and immediately called an ambulance, which came to pick Arthur up on the side of the road and conceivably saved his life. Arthur was transported to the Mayo Clinic in Rochester, Minnesota, and eventually got back into military control hospitalization.

"An Officer and a Gentleman": Richard Gere balked at shooting the ending of the film, in which Zack arrives at Paula's factory wearing his naval dress whites and carries her off the factory floor. Gere thought the ending would not work because it was too sentimental. Director Taylor Hackford agreed with Gere until, during a rehearsal, the extras playing the workers began to cheer and cry. When Gere saw the scene later, with a portion of the score (that was used to write "Up Where We Belong") played at the right tempo, he said it gave him chills. Gere is now convinced Hackford made the right decision. [21] Screenwriter Michael Hauge, in his book, Writing Screenplays That Sell, echoed this opinion:

Tam at finish line!

Very Proud Pop!

"I don't believe that those who criticized this Cinderella-style ending were paying very close attention to who exactly is rescuing whom." [citation needed] From Wikipedia, the free encyclopedia.

My new British Lady was too Cute!

"Scroll through any social-media feed, and before long a cute video will appear. Perhaps it shows a giggling baby or a rabbit nibbling strawberries. A red panda might be throwing its paws in the air, like a furry thief being apprehended, or a kitten may sit astride a tiny motorcycle. The supply of these endearing clips is huge. On TikTok, there are 65m videos tagged #cute. The demand is even greater. Those videos have been viewed more than 625b times. Cute things are everywhere, not just online. In Japan, where appreciation for all things kawaii is especially keen, roadblocks come in the form of dolphins, ducks, or frogs. Hello Kitty, a cartoon, adorns everything from phone chargers to first-aid kits. In America, a puppy has advertised beer, and an endearing gecko helps GEICO sell around $39b in car insurance a year." (Economist)

Arthur did indeed meet his cute British girlfriend when she was studying French and working at the local commissary on the same post where Arthur was stationed. Although he did not actually lift her up physically like in the movie, he did ask her to join him in Kansas when he was transferred there as part of "Operation Reforger". She did indeed go along, and eventually, they were happily married at Fort Riley, Kansas, where he was then a Captain and Company Commander, NATO. It was a lovely start to a love life with his British wife, leading to a wonderful life in Great Britain.

Life in Great Britain with his new wonderful Dutch wife and two lovely daughters, Hampshire, was the best! Horse riding, bike riding, walking, and exploring the countryside were among the activities they enjoyed. Their daughters were part of the swim team in Surrey and engaged in a number of lovely activities toward admission to two wonderful universities and eventual teaching opportunities as well.

Hampshire is also home to the now world-famous Highclere Castle, thanks to its starring role as Downton Abbey. It has become one of England's most visited destinations. Open to the public between July and September, visitors can explore the Jacobean manor house with its ornately decorated rooms. For the ultimate Downton treat, booking a stay in an on-site lodge allows one to soak in the morning views of one of England's most iconic houses.

For Arthur, London was a springboard after teaching there in 2003 and 2004, while the children attended school at delightful Midhurst. Then, in 2007, he taught in Geneva, Switzerland, and they loved living in Epesse Switzerland and Villars, after which they drove to Benbowpond in West Sussex and then to the Netherlands. All a wonderful journey with more to come!

Note to former colleagues.

"Hope you are well! Are you alright! That's the way the British greet you here. Yes I did get your docs thanks. Don't really need to receive them by mail, but here is my new address for future reference: **Broomhill Cottage, Benbow Pond Cowdray Park Cottages,** Midhurst, West Sussex, GU29 0AQ United Kingdom Telephone Number Home: Broomhill: 01730-814905 The sun came out today as well. It was a total horse day, as we went to the Riding for the Disabled to help out. Very nice organization to help children connect with other living things, in this case horses. But the sky was blue too. So all is good. Very nice people, the Brits. Now I know where you got it. All the best."

Polo Ground 007

"Penny Churchill takes a look at **Conford Park House,** a beautiful Arts-and-Crafts home in Hampshire that's been extensively modernised. Conford Park House, a classic Arts-and-Crafts house in East Hampshire, sits in 50 acres of beautifully landscaped gardens, grounds, paddocks and woodland." See Visit England and Highclere Park, Newbury RG20 9RN

For Arthur, a poor boy originally from Los Angeles, The prospect of being face-to-face **within feet of the royal family of England,** and likewise, the royal players of polo, would've never occurred to me as something that would happen in my life.

Because I was teaching in London and my children were at school and Midhurst Elementary school we were directly across the street from the polo grounds Cowdrey polo grounds. Dear Dominique earned a wonderful honor there as well as the numerous awards that both lovely daughters earned! So Proud! LABOR OXINIA WINCIT Midhurst Grammar School Founder's Day Prize 2004 Awarded To Dominique De La Loza SUBJECT PRIZE for Modern Languages Mr Colin Hughes, Chairman of Midhurst Town Council, Midhurst Resources Centre & the Cowdray Heritage Project. Duke of Edinburgh Award Scheme Co-ordinator for the Midhurst Youth Wing. (Midhurst Grammar School 1968 -2001). Mr J Stringer Chairman of Govermors.

She wrote a paper on Hadley Grange where a famous singer composed a famous song:

Headley Grange is a former workhouse in Headley, Hampshire, England. It is a Grade II listed historic building. It is best known for its use as a recording and rehearsal venue in the 1960s and 1970s, by acts including Led Zeppelin, Genesis, Bad Company, and Help Yourself. Parts of Led Zeppelin's albums Led Zeppelin III, Led Zeppelin IV, Houses of the Holy, and Physical Graffiti were composed and/or recorded at Headley Grange. Led Zeppelin vocalist Robert Plant wrote most of the lyrics to Led Zeppelin's "Stairway to Heaven" there in a single day. The Led Zeppelin song "Black Dog," which, like "Stairway," appeared on Led Zeppelin IV, was named after a black Labrador Retriever which was found hanging around Headley Grange during recording. [From Wikipedia, the free encyclopedia.]

I suspect that my lovely Dutch wife, who was a horse lover and rode horses as a fancy dressage rider, selected our home because of the polo grounds right across the street. Whenever there was an event, I used to put on my polo clothes and boots and drive my car onto the polo grounds, a

Mercedes SL 450 convertible. I would then park it with all the other fancy cars and walk through the grounds, mingling with the horse riders and polo players. Latin Americans were considered the "best" according to the Queen, so I fit in perfectly!

Dressage is a sport involving the execution of precise movements by a trained horse in response to barely perceptible signals from its rider. The word dressage means "training" in French. Particularly important are the animal's pace and bearing in performing walks, trots, canters, and more specialized maneuvers.

The Gracida brothers were the world's most famous and best polo players, according to the Queen. Prince Charles and his sons were also playing, and there was a box made up of a simple picket fence about 2 to 3 feet high where the royal family sat on the other side. When I bought a bottle of champagne and walked by, I would say good day. I had my champagne bottle with me and my fancy champagne drinking glass, and I would pour a little bit here and there for anyone who wanted to join in. It was a delightful experience, and I got to be face-to-face with royalty, something I never dreamed would happen.

https://www.google.com/search?client=safari&sca_esv=27b000d398e4e776&hl=en-us&q=Gracida+polo&sa=X&ved=2ahUKEwjmsa-S_o2FAxU8JEQIHeLoAPgQ1QJ6BAgPEAI&biw=278&bih=529&dpr=3 ARTHUR

Gracida was ranked 9 goals in England, where he was reportedly HM Queen Elizabeth's favorite player. He was a favorite instructor with celebrities and royalty and gave lessons to HRH Prince Charles, HRH Prince William, HRH Prince Harry, King Constantine II of Greece, HRH Prince Talal of Jordan, James Packer and Sylvester Stallone. [1]

Arthur Fitting in at Cowdrey Polo Grounds with Carlos Gracida - "best" according to the Queen!

Of note is the first impression at the school: the drinking age was so low that it was the first time I saw wine being poured and drunk by young people at school. When my kids first got to Midhurst Elementary School, they heard the children there saying "I can't be bothered" when it came to homework. That was the first time they ever heard that - amazing! It was fun!

Midhurst is a market town, parish, and civil parish in West Sussex, England. It lies on the River Rother 20 miles inland from the English Channel and 12 miles north of the county town of Chichester. The name Midhurst was first recorded in 1186 as Middeherst, meaning "Middle wooded hill" or "among the wooded hills." (Wikipedia)

Midhurst is a market town, parish and civil parish in West Sussex, England. It lies on the River Rother 20 miles inland from the English Channel, and 12 miles north of the county town of Chichester. The name Midhurst was first recorded in 1186 as Middeherst, meaning "Middle wooded hill", or among the wooded hills". Wikipedia

We visited Hadley Grange, a place of musical significance where my daughter wrote a paper. It's known for its association with Led Zeppelin, where they wrote and recorded significant portions of their albums, including "Stairway to Heaven" in a single day. The Led Zeppelin song "Black Dog," which also appeared on the album Led Zeppelin IV, was named after a black Labrador Retriever found hanging around Headley Grange during recording. (From Wikipedia, the free encyclopedia)

We loved our family time in the wonderful urban area of Haslemere!

Much of the civil parish is in the catchment area of the south branch of the River Wey, which rises on Blackdown in West Sussex. The urban areas of Haslemere and Shottermill are concentrated along the valleys of the young river and its tributaries, and many of the local roads are narrow and steep. The National Trust is a major landowner in the civil parish, and its properties include Swan Barn Farm. The Surrey Hills Area of Outstanding Natural Beauty is to the north of the town, and the South Downs National Park is to the south.

Haslemere is thought to have originated as a planned town in the 12th century and was awarded a market charter in 1221. By the early 16th century, it had become a Parliamentary borough and was represented by two MPs in the House of Commons until 1832. The town began to grow in the second half of the 19th century, following the opening of the London to Portsmouth railway line in 1859. In late-Victorian times, it became a center for the Arts and Crafts movement, and the International Dolmetsch Early Music Festival was founded in 1925.

Haslemere became an Urban District in 1913, but under the Local Government Act 1972, its status was reduced to a civil parish with a town council.

The town of Haslemere (/ˈhæzlˌmɪər/) and the villages of Shottermill and Grayswood are in southwest Surrey, England, around 38 miles (62 km) southwest of London. Together with the settlements of Hindhead and Beacon Hill, they comprise the civil parish of Haslemere in the Borough of Waverley. The tripoint between the counties of Surrey, Hampshire, and West Sussex is at the west end of Shottermill. (Wikipedia)

First Days in US Army!

Promotion!

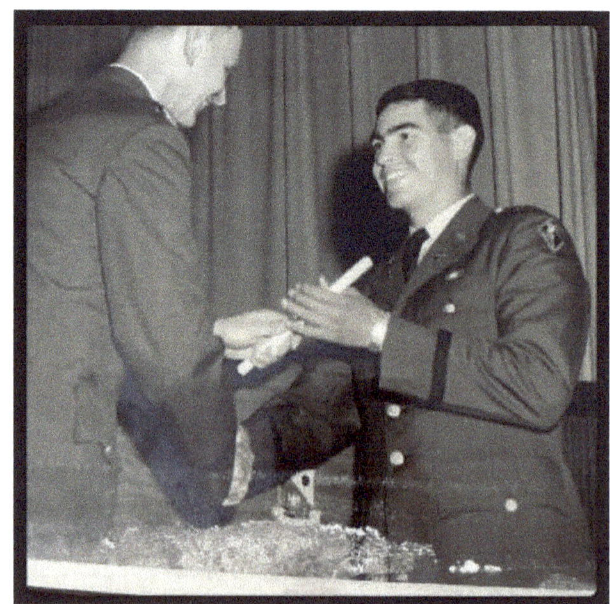

Officer Candidate School!

Love at First Sight: Meeting a Lovely British Lady in Augsburg, Germany

After completing his Officer Candidate School program at Aberdeen, Maryland, it was his first night on the town in Germany. He walked up to a lovely lady waiting for a bus on the street corner and said, "Excuse me, do you speak English?" She looked at him with her beautiful blue eyes and replied, "I am English." Arthur was immediately in love because she was so perfect and had the most beautiful eyes he had ever seen. He said to himself, "She's going to help me get over the sad loss of my darling girlfriend, living in Beverly Hills, California. Renee." Corinne (Renee) had recently visited another naval officer training location in the United States to meet up with her lieutenant Navy boyfriend! He then asked, "I'm looking for a club called the Big Apple, can you tell me where it is?" She said yes and told him exactly where it was, giving Arthur directions with her lovely British accent. This encounter was the reason he became so enamored with England, the culture, and the beauty of Great Britain when he first arrived with her some years later. It was around 6 PM in Augsburg, Bavaria, Germany. When the young Second Lieutenant Arthur, having just been deployed, walked up to a beautiful lady waiting for a bus in the downtown area and said, "Do you speak English?" falling in love with her beautiful blue eyes, she replied, with a gorgeous English accent, "I am English." This would be the beginning of all of the loveliest chapters in Arthur's life. He then asked, "Do you know what the Big Apple is?" She said yes, it's just down the street and on the left-hand side.

Arthur just arrived in Bavaria, having lived the most fun years of his life in Hollywood on the corner of **Melrose and Vine,** attending and enjoying wonderful places like the Whisky a Go Go, and PJs where he danced the night away with lovely and exciting ladies. This was his "Once upon a time in Hollywood" experience. **"Once Upon a Time... in Hollywood" is a 2019 comedy-drama film** written and directed by Quentin Tarantino. Produced by Columbia Pictures, Bona Film Group, Heyday Films, and Visiona Romantica, and distributed by Sony Pictures Releasing, it is a co-production between the United States, United Kingdom, and China. The film features a large ensemble cast led by Leonardo DiCaprio, Brad Pitt, and Margot Robbie. Set in 1969 Los Angeles, the film follows a fading actor and his stunt double as they navigate the rapidly changing film industry, with the looming threat of the Tate murders hanging overhead. It features "multiple storylines in a modern fairy tale tribute to the final moments of Hollywood's golden age." (From Wikipedia, the free encyclopedia)

British Lady Love: He would soon meet up with this lovely English lady, ask her to dance, and love her very modest dance moves compared to the incredible dancing he experienced in Hollywood. Years later, after having been together for some time, they would watch the movie "An Officer and a Gentleman" with tears in their eyes, reminiscing about their time in Germany while he was in the service and she was working at one of the military commissaries or supermarkets while studying French there. "An Officer and a Gentleman" is a 1982 American romantic drama film directed by Taylor Hackford from a screenplay by Douglas Day Stewart, and starring Richard Gere, Debra Winger, and Louis Gossett Jr. It tells the story of Zack Mayo (Gere), a United States Navy Aviation Officer Candidate beginning his training at Aviation Officer Candidate School. While Zack meets his first true girlfriend during his training, a young "townie named Paula (Winger)." (From Wikipedia, the free encyclopedia).

He was in the 7th Army:

George Smith Patton Jr. was a general in the United States Army who commanded the Seventh United States Army in the Mediterranean Theater of World War II, and the Third United States Army in France and Germany after the Allied invasion of Normandy in June 1944. Wikipedia -

On 30th November 1966, the Seventh Army was relocated from Patch Barracks to Heidelberg. Following French disagreements with certain NATO policies, United States European Command relocated from Paris the following year. From that time forward, the Seventh Army has been the headquarters for all Army units under the European Command. Its major subordinate elements were the V Corps and VII Corps (Inactivated 1992.) From 1 December 1966 to the present, the commander of Seventh Army has been "dual-hatted as Commanding General, United States Army Europe.

From Army to Love at First Sight:

This chapter was the beginning of Arthur's incredible British journey, eventually leading to his loving teaching as a professor of international law at the wonderful campus located in London at Regents Park and Cowdrey Park Polo. That chapter in his grateful life as a professor found him teaching in London and living with his family in West Sussex Hampshire county. At that time, the thankful professor and his children were very close to the lovely town of Midhurst, where his children attended school located directly across the street from Kari Park. The polo grounds where he and his family were able to watch Prince Charles and his sons play polo.

Arthur was a fan of Polo and riding horses, so he would put on his polo outfits, along with the boots and knee pads, purchase a bottle of champagne, and walk up to the royal box to toast the royal family as they watched Prince Charles and his sons play polo, along with the famous Gracida brothers from Mexico. This teaching experience in London led to another chapter, which found him in Switzerland living in the Alps and teaching in Geneva.

"Geneva is a city in Switzerland that lies at the southern tip of expansive Lac Léman (Lake Geneva). Surrounded by **the Alps and Jura mountains, the city has views of dramatic Mont Blanc.**

Headquarters of Europe's United Nations and the Red Cross, it's a global hub for diplomacy and banking. French influence is widespread, from the language to gastronomy and bohemian districts like Carouge." - Google

By then, Arthur was an attorney from the wonderful city of Newport Beach, California, and found himself blessed to be able to teach at the legal capital of the world, The Hague, Netherlands, for five years. This thankful journey resulted in Arthur creating a new course for graduate and undergraduate students called **Comparative US, EU law.** He and his new students would travel from London to Brussels to Bruges to Amsterdam, and then to Paris. This program was so successful and appreciated by the schools and students that he created another one from Venice to Nice to Montecarlo, Florence, and then to Rome. Arthur even received a thank you letter from the University President and accolades from students and their parents.

On to Lovely England: We loved our time near Leith Hill in southern England. It is the highest summit of the Greensand Ridge, approximately 6.7 km southwest of Dorking, Surrey, and 40.5 km southwest of central London. It reaches 294 m above sea level and is the second-highest point in southeast England, after Walbury Hill in southwest Berkshire. Cowdray Park Holiday Cottages, Heathend Cottage, Cowdray Park, Midhurst, West Sussex GU290AQ, United Kingdom!

It was a nice 10-hour drive from Geneva for Mommy and me. We had a long day yesterday when we went to Geneva to pick up the other car. Then we drove part of the way to Dijon and spent the night in a nice hotel. We are now back at that place we stayed at when we first left, called Cowdray Holiday Cottages. Really very nice upgrades since we were here last, and it looks all new inside. We finally pulled in about 9:00 PM after driving 10 hours.

The park lies in the South Downs National Park. The estate belongs to Viscount Cowdray, whose family have owned it since 1909. It has a golf course, and it offers clay pigeon shooting and corporate activity days, as well as the more traditional activities of agriculture, forestry, and property lets.

While in the army during Boot Camp, I had a picture of my girlfriend in my locker, Renee, who lived in Beverly Hills - and during an inspection, the sergeant looked in there and said, "What's that?" I said, "That's my girlfriend, I love her," because he said, "Why do you have that?" and I said, "Because I love her," and he said, **"Love is only found in the dictionary between lunacy and leprosy." So much for military training!**

Black pool

offers something for everyone. An abundance of award-winning attractions, six miles of beach, a huge selection of accommodation, and an exciting annual program of free events for all the family to enjoy! Since the 1800s, Blackpool has been Britain's most popular seaside resort. With entertainment at the very heart of everything we do, the resort is synonymous with fun-filled and action-packed adventures for all the family.

2024 is shaping up to be one of the best years yet, with a diary packed full of fun and promise for all to enjoy. Thrill-seekers can enjoy the thrills and spills of the white-knuckle rides at Blackpool Pleasure Beach or feel the thrills of a bygone era on one of the oldest amusement rides in Europe,

Sir Hiram Maxim's Captive Flying Machines. Don't forget to take a trip to the world-famous Blackpool Tower, one of the most loved and recognizable landmarks in the world and home to the stunning Blackpool Tower Ballroom, The Blackpool Tower Circus, The Blackpool Tower Eye, and The Blackpool Tower Dungeons, all under one roof.

Those looking for an animal-mad adventure can visit Blackpool Zoo or take a swim with the sharks at SEA LIFE Blackpool. Meet the stars and mingle with royalty at Madame Tussauds, or for a more chilled-out afternoon, take a dip in the 84-degree sub-tropical paradise at Sandcastle Waterpark. The world-famous Blackpool Illuminations need little introduction. With six miles of traditional festoons, tableaux, and interactive features along the Promenade, it's commonly known as the greatest free light show on Earth! Blackpool's annual Illuminations display shines nightly from the beginning of September into the Christmas season. Never a destination to stand still, Blackpool's latest attraction, Showtown, will open in March 2024.

This £13m museum aims to celebrate Blackpool's internationally significant story as the UK's most popular seaside destination, along with its role in the development of British popular culture. Open year-round, the brand-new museum will be fun, accessible, and fully immersive, filled with objects, film, music, and performance.

Westminster Abbey, located just west of the Houses of Parliament in the Greater London London borough of Westminster, my family and students loved this during or times and visits to London is a church that serves as the site of coronations and other ceremonies of national significance. Situated on the grounds of a former Benedictine monastery, it was refounded as the Collegiate Church of St. Peter in Westminster by Queen Elizabeth I in 1560. In 1987, Westminster Abbey, St. Margaret's Church, and the Houses of Parliament were collectively designated as a UNESCO World Heritage Site.

After Arthur first met his future British wife, as luck would have it, they both met again at The Big Apple a couple of days later, where they danced the night away. It was during this time that he learned she was working at the commissary on the same post where he was stationed. This marked the beginning of Arthur's wonderful experience with Great Britain, England, and his future teaching assignment in London.

Years later. British wife reminded him, "We met at Koenigsplatz bus stop when I was leaving my German class at the Berlin School of Languages. Yes, I was working at the Commissary as well. You used to pick me up from there at the end of my shift." It was evident that Arthur was fully committed to their relationship.

As time passes, Arthur expresses gratitude for experiencing new things and places. He finds joy in teaching new students and receiving great reviews from them, regardless of their location. Despite challenges such as dragging his suitcase uphill through snow in the Swiss Alps or navigating the intricate train stations in England, Arthur remains physically fit and determined to keep moving and exploring.

With friends returning from places like Morocco and invitations to visit Saudi Arabia from students, Arthur acknowledges the vastness of the world and the limited time available to explore it all. Nonetheless, he remains eager to continue his adventures and discover more.

Meeting some very interesting people. One of our first neighbors was from the World Bank, and another was recently the Energy Advisor to many Middle Eastern countries, so it is all interesting. There are many United Nations Diplomats in Geneva, and the students are very well connected too.

Here in the UK, I have a desire to write a book on the origins of the common law and how it has evolved to our new concepts based on necessity. In Switzerland, we were in the French part, and the natives were very happy if you started trying to speak French, as they disliked the English who never even tried at all. That motivated me to be able to do most simple things in French like shopping and going to restaurants. "But my Dutch wife was the best because she could do it all." She would pick it up for me when they all started to rattle on in French. Dominique did very well too because she has studied it for eight years and gets it from her mom.

Tamara spoke a little French, and she and all her friends from the States and England would go out each night and meet up with guys from all over the world. It was safe because we were in a place called Villars, where some of the best international schools in the world are located. But they all did well speaking different languages, including Spanish. However, the common language is English when in mixed company, so it is not bad at all.

The last party we went to in Switzerland was attended by people of all nationalities, and they were all kind enough to speak English with us, so that was fine. The hardest people to understand are the Brits. It's like a foreign language until you get the hang of it again.

To my friends:

Hi Catherine and Peter,

We are in the English Countryside with all the polo ponies. And you, as a rider, would love it! The ponies are right behind us on the hillside, and all the players from Mexico and Argentina are coming for world-class competition. They practice in March. The Gracida brothers are the "Best" according to the Queen!

To our great friends:

Hi All, And Jan especially,

How cool to see all your email addresses at once. Irma and I are in The Netherlands after a year in the Swiss Alps and half a year in the UK. I miss you all, but Webster.nl made me an offer I could not refuse, so three days a week I am the Head of Business in Leiden, near the World Court in The Hague and near Irma's Mom's place. We love it, and the kids come to visit. We are now settled in a cottage right next to the Polo grounds, with super bike trails and walking trails, and of course, Irma's favorite: lots of horses. You should come for a visit and stay with us. We have an extra bedroom with a bath and shower ensuite, and you two can be totally private. We will pick you up at the airport. We are booked until the end of April, but will get another place close by since Polo competition will really start by then. Irma is riding now and helping with riding for the disabled, which she loves.

From Beautiful Switzerland to lovely Great Britain:

We lived in this great place while Arthur was teaching in Geneva!

Villars-sur-Ollon is a village in the western Swiss Vaud Alps. Trails include the Bretaye to Ollon route, with views of Lake Geneva, vineyards, and the Leysin ski resort. A cable car from Col du Pillon ascends to Les Diablerets Massif, home to the Glacier 3000 mountain station, Peak Walk suspension bridge, and Matterhorn views. To the south, Bex has a working salt mine and a narrow-gauge railway connecting it to Aigle.

Arthur will be teaching an EU class in May including London, Brugge, Brussels, Amsterdam, and Paris! We will send some info in case you want to join in the fun. It would be a great 9-day party.

My daughter Tamara: is now teaching internationally. After Summer 2005 Stanford University, Junior Statesmen of America- Honors Diploma, along with many other accomplishments! Very proud!

Dominique did her A Levels while in the UK: Advanced level qualifications (known as A levels) are subject-based qualifications that can lead to university, further study, training, or work. You can normally study three or more A levels over two years. They're usually assessed by a series of examinations.

Dominique also did her SAT exam near a famous place: Abbey Road is a thoroughfare in the borough of Camden and the City of Westminster in Greater London running roughly northwest to southeast through St John's Wood near Lord's Cricket Ground. It is part of the road B507.

EDITOR'S LETTER: What does quintessential England look like to you? In this issue, I found it in the unspoilt villages and market towns of Wiltshire (p64), a place positively brimming with country pubs and thatched cottages. For many, it's London's iconic sights that stir the soul, none more so than Tower Bridge (p30), surely one of the world's most-loved landmarks. Or perhaps it's the image of punts gliding alongside the backs of Cambridge's colleges that has you dreaming of a quintessential English summer (p75). You'll find them all within the pages of this issue. We also pay a visit to Cheshire, whose quieter charms are well worth exploring (p14), and in our ancestry piece discover the past lives of three National Trust buildings, both above and below stairs (p54). If you've ever wondered what secrets lie in your own family tree, we have all the tips for you to get started. And with a new season of Bridgerton on its way, we dance through the history of the debutante ball, an aristocratic rite of passage for 'debs' in search of a suitable husband (p23). Enjoy the issue!

England's countryside is renowned for its timeless beauty, picturesque landscapes, and tranquil charm. For those seeking a break from the bustle of city life or looking to immerse themselves in the idyllic charms of the English countryside, exploring the rural regions is an absolute must. From rolling green hills to quaint villages, this subchapter highlights the captivating allure of rural England, providing a glimpse into the essence of countryside living.

One of the most enchanting aspects of rural England is its breathtaking landscapes. The countryside is adorned with undulating hills, endless meadows, and meandering rivers that paint a soothing and captivating backdrop. These landscapes offer a haven for outdoor enthusiasts, with a plethora of activities such as hiking, cycling, and horseback riding. From the expansive Yorkshire Dales to the mystical beauty of the Cotswolds, each region boasts its charm and beauty! This is a quote from another Designer project I'm working on!

Conford Park is where we lived while I was teaching in London.

We were in a beautiful hamlet just 50 miles outside of London and loved every minute of it. It was just over the cute little lake and waterway that you had to cross in order to get to our cottage, nestled in the hillside. There were even deer running up to the back window to look into our kitchen to see what we were up to. There were also horses living next door, so it was a wonderful environment, especially for my wife, who is a lovely horse rider and enjoys dressage.

"When you're planning school trips abroad, it's important to conduct thorough research about the destination. If you spend only some time looking for places, you'll realize that London is one of the most popular destinations for school trips. With a school travel company, you don't have to worry about planning an overseas school trip. The company takes care of everything and ensures that your kids have a wonderful learning experience.

School trips to London offer numerous benefits, and some of them have been discussed in this post. London is one of the best locations for school tours. Every year, the city attracts millions of tourists from around the world. In 2012, London even hosted the Olympic Games, a global event that put it on the map for educational and field tours. Since then, schools from every part of the world have taken trips to London in search of learning experiences.

London is considered to be a world city and features some of the most amazing educational sights, such as churches, law courts, parliament, museums, historical landmarks, and more. During a visit to London, students will also be able to witness culture from around the world. In addition to this, the southeastern side of England has several venues focused on school groups. Students can visit campuses of some heritage London schools, art galleries, residential activity centers, and museums, most of which cover a broad spectrum of subjects in the curriculum. Whether your students would be interested in Roman history or Victorian England, school trips to London provide them with a chance to witness everything up-close.

When it comes to school trips abroad, London is perhaps the best choice. With so much to offer, it provides an unmatched learning experience to kids."

The historic Greenwich meridian is a geographical reference line that passes through the Royal

Observatory, Greenwich, in London, England. The modern IERS Reference Meridian widely used today is based on the Greenwich meridian.

WHITE CLIFFS OF DOVER

An iconic landmark, the spectacular 100m-high White Cliffs overlook the English Channel; the perfect place for breathtaking coastal path walks.

CANTERBURY

This charming city impresses with stunning architecture and a rich history. Admire the oldest cathedral in England, walk in the footsteps of Chaucer's medieval pilgrims, or wander the narrow medieval alleys.

OXFORD

This distinguished university city, one of the oldest seats of learning in the world, has honey-colored buildings, magnificent historic colleges, and cobbled streets. Best enjoyed from a punt on the River Cherwell.

RYE

With its cobbled streets and timber-framed buildings, the medieval town of Rye is pretty as a picture. There's lots to see, from the 13th-century Rye Castle to Lamb House, the home of author Henry James.

WINDSOR CASTLE

Windsor Castle has seen a thousand years of history and has served as a home to 39 monarchs. It was used as Queen Elizabeth II's main residence. You can visit St. George's Chapel and the opulent state apartments, and see the Changing of the Guard.

BRIGHTON

A cool seaside town known for its iconic pier and shopping in the famous Lanes. The Brighton Pavilion, George IV's extravagant palace, is a must-visit.

GARDENS OF KENT

Kent's High Weald has a generous sprinkling of some of England's greatest gardens, including Vita Sackville-West's Sissinghurst and exuberant Great Dixter.

HAMPTON COURT PALACE

Explore the extravagant interiors of the Baroque palace that was once Henry VII's favorite, from the Great Hall to the Tudor Kitchen, before getting lost in the UK's oldest surviving hedge maze.

MARGATE

Trendy Margate has a broad sandy beach, the Turner Contemporary gallery, and a quirky old town.

WINCHESTER

Winchester is a handsome market town with an abundance of history. Visit King Arthur's Round Table and go on the Jane Austen trail: the novelist was born in nearby Chawton.

SOUTHEAST ENGLAND

Much of southeast England is an easy train ride from London but seems a world away. The area, which takes in Berkshire, Buckinghamshire, Hampshire, the Isle of Wight, Kent, Oxfordshire, Surrey, and Sussex, is characterized by countryside, coast, and charm. Seaside resorts have a creative vibe. Margate in Kent is home to Tuner Contemporary, a leading art gallery built on the site of a boarding house that used to host JMW Turner. Brighton in East Sussex has the spectacular Royal Pavilion, with its domes and minarets. Visitors while away whole days milling around country estates and gardens, from Sissinghurst in Kent, renovated by the writer Vita Sackville-West, to grand Cliveden House, on the Buckinghamshire-Berkshire border, which has been home to one prince of Wales, two dukes, and an earl. For more royal history, there's magnificent Windsor Castle. The Prince and Princess of Wales, William and Kate, live in a cottage on-site.

Kazakhstan Celebration Day, Oct. 5th.jpg

The importance of education can never be overestimated. They say that "to teach is to change lives forever." Yet, of most importance is that if you look around at all the people in the world that you come in contact with, they are all teachers, in one way or another! From the "essential workers" who sacrifice so much, especially during the recent pandemic, such as the hospital workers, the pharmacy workers, the supermarket workers, and teachers, as well as all those who kept education at the forefront of lives by providing books at the local bookstore and help when someone was looking for what they needed to complete their lives. We all can learn much just by observing, and realizing that these wonderful men and women are changing lives on a daily basis. In ways that can "Never be taken away!"

One of the ways I frequently started my classes was by asking the following question: "If you had unlimited resources, and money were no object, what would you do with your life?" Many of my students would answer that they would travel and see the world. My most important "icing on the cake" of my entire teaching experience was the creation of a course called "Comparative United States - European Union Law." This was the course where I traveled with my students from London to Brussels, Bruges, Amsterdam, and Paris - and then again from Venice to Nice, Monte Carlo, to Florence and Rome, and then back to Venice! And in doing so, my hope and prayer is that this education which can "never be taken away" did indeed change the lives of my students! And that this life experience was an education for me and all the students I came in contact with, that can in closing "never be taken away" to use the words of my Father when I was a young child selling newspapers on the corner and shining shoes.

With heartfelt thanks, gratitude, and love to all the teachers in my life, starting with my parents, family members, and school teachers that I learned from my entire life, I devote this work and recollection of my global journey as evidence that teachers in every way **changed my life forever**.

God Bless!

Many years later, after meeting this lovely British woman, Arthur earned his LL.M. in taxation at Golden Gate University after having served in the US military - NATO-deployed to Germany as an Army Captain and Company Commander. Then, after his tour of duty, he moved on to work as a Bank Officer for United California Bank, then managing the City Treasurer's office at the City of Huntington Beach, CA, eventually becoming a Deputy City Attorney, where he led and participated in the largest municipal bankruptcy case in the history of the United States, winning a large sum of money on behalf of his client, the City of Huntington Beach, and other public entities similarly situated.

Then, Arthur decided to continue his education with other working adults at Golden Gate University. He was blessed to have a wonderful wife from the Netherlands, and the study of International Taxation was important to him. Eventually, he went on to live in the Netherlands while teaching globally as a university professor, offering courses in International Law and Taxation for Webster University, teaching at Regents Park in London, then Geneva, and then N.L. near the Hague, known as "the Legal Capital of the World."

In the Netherlands, Arthur created a travel study undergraduate and graduate course called "Comparative US/EU Law." He took students from London to Brussels, Bruges, Amsterdam, and then to Paris. This was such a success that he created another course, traveling from Venice to Nice, Monte Carlo, Florence, and then Rome, and back to Venice.

Arthur has always been thankful and very grateful for his teachers, professors, military instructors, and other professionals throughout his life, as well as his parents, who instilled in him the true value and life meaning of books. His father's words, "Son, get an education; they can never take it away from you," have proven to be true. The fact that Golden Gate University catered to working adults was a perfect match for him and those of his future students similarly situated, inspiring all who participated.

Now, Arthur is writing a book about his gratitude to all who inspired him, including his fellow students and professors at Golden Gate University. He looks forward to sharing more about his journey when the book is published in the next 30-69 days.

Arthur expresses his heartfelt thanks and gratitude to Shirley and others who have supported him along the way. He reflects on his experiences teaching all over Europe, receiving warm welcomes, and attending many events designed for ambassadors from other countries, especially in Wassenaar, Netherlands. He was even invited to meet special people like the Ambassador from India, who invited him to his home to meet other ambassadors from around the world.

Lovely Dutch Wife!

Some of the Ambassadors were kind enough to accept my invitation to give presentations at the World Trade Center in Amsterdam for the organization I developed in the Netherlands - "The Center for the Advancement of Women and Diversity in Business" (see videos on YouTube). My two lovely daughters even attended and ultimately became teachers as well due to this wonderful exposure, supported by their Dutch mom. They attended school at Midhurst Elementary while I was teaching in London. At one point, we even watched Prince Charles and his sons play polo at Cowdray Park Polo Club Sports Club in Easebourne, England, directly across the street from their school in Midhurst, the United Kingdom, when I was teaching in London. Consequently, I've always been thankful and very grateful for my teachers and professors, my military instructors, and other professionals throughout my life, as well as my parents who purchased an Encyclopedia Britannica at a time when we could scarcely afford food and taught us the true value and life meaning of books. My father said to me, "Son, get an education they can never take away from you." Clearly, he was correct. The fact that Golden Gate University catered to working adults was

a perfect match for me and those of my future students similarly situated, inspiring all who participated, especially me. One class I had was in downtown Los Angeles, very close to the corner where I used to shine shoes and sell newspapers as a poor boy, who now lives in one of the wealthiest parts of California, Newport Beach, where my clients parked their yachts in front of my waterfront office at Lido Marina Village. I'm now writing a book about my thanks to all who inspired me, including Golden Gate University fellow students, and professors alike - much more to come later when it is published in the next 30-69 days.

Shirley, thanks for the note. Looks like you will indeed be at my favorite places in Greece. My wife is Dutch, so it was a natural extension for me to focus my post-doctorate LL.M. on international taxation, which led to teaching international law and then the travel-study courses. We also lived in the UK back in 2003-2004 when I taught at Webster London, another great place to be. But if you specialize in an area, even art history or such, you can tie it into a course with a travel-study program. I'll keep you posted on any new courses as they materialize. You should go to the passports.com site and see if there are some ideas for London will be my focus of attention here, since that was my start after leaving "The O.C." for my travel and teaching journey!

In the Netherlands, some of the ambassadors were kind enough to accept my invitation to give presentations at the World Trade Center in Amsterdam for the organization I developed in the Netherlands - "The Center for the Advancement of Women and Diversity in Business" (see videos on YouTube). My two lovely daughters even attended and ultimately became teachers as well due to this wonderful exposure, supported by their very supportive Dutch mom.

Loved our wedding:

In the Netherlands, some of the ambassadors were kind enough to accept my invitation to give presentations at the World Trade Center in Amsterdam for the organization I developed in the Netherlands - "The Center for the Advancement of Women and Diversity in Business" (see videos on YouTube). My two lovely daughters even attended and ultimately became teachers as well due to this wonderful exposure, supported by their very supportive Dutch mom.

BEAUTIFUL DUTCH WIFE AND MOMMY OF MY DARLING DAUGHTERS!

Consequently, I've always been thankful and very grateful for my teachers, professors, military instructors, and other professionals throughout my life. I'm also deeply appreciative of my parents, who purchased an Encyclopedia Britannica at a time when we could scarcely afford food, teaching us the true value and life meaning of books. My father's advice to me, "son, get an education they can never take away from you," was profoundly correct. The fact that Golden Gate University catered to working adults was a perfect match for me, and for my future students similarly situated. It inspired all who participated, especially me. One class I had was in downtown Los Angeles, very close to the corner where I used to shine shoes and sell newspapers as a poor boy. Now, I live in one of the wealthiest parts of California, Newport Beach, where my clients park their yachts in front of my waterfront office at Lido Marina Village. Even John Wayne's yacht could be seen from my office. While many stars from Orange County have been important, none could ever be truly as great as the iconic actor John Wayne. Born as Marion Morrison, The Duke moved to California from Iowa as a child and was noticed by John Ford when he was working as an assistant on a movie studio. He starred in more than 150 films, with many of them directed by Ford. He is an iconic actor best known for his roles in western movies like "Stagecoach" and "True Grit". He lived in Newport Harbor in Newport Beach and enjoyed sailing on his old yacht along the shores of the city in Orange County. Today, the main Orange County airport is named in honor of John Wayne. A massive bronze sculpture of him is seen near my office.

I'm now writing this book to express my gratitude to all who inspired me, including international students and professors alike. Much more will come later!

Midhurst was wonderful! Quintessential Britain!

Midhurst (/ˈmɪdhərst/) is a market town, parish, and civil parish in West Sussex, England. It lies on the River Rother 20 miles (32 km) inland from the English Channel and 12 miles (19 km) north of the county town of Chichester. The name Midhurst was first recorded in 1186 as Middeherst, meaning "Middle wooded hill" or "(place) among the wooded hills". It derives from the Old English words midd (adjective) or mid (preposition), meaning "in the middle", plus hyrst, "a wooded hill". The Norman St. Ann's Castle dates from about 1120, although only the foundations remain visible. The castle, the parish church of St. Mary Magdalene and St. Denis, together with South Pond, the former fish-pond for the castle, are the only three structures left from this early period. The parish church is the oldest building in Midhurst. Just across the River Rother, in the parish of Easebourne, is the ruin of the Tudor Cowdray House.

Consequently I've always been thankful and very grateful for my teachers and professors, my military instructors and other professionals all through life, as well as my parents who purchased an encyclopedia Britannica at a time when we could scarcely afford food and taught us the true value and life meaning of books.

My father said to me, "son, get an education they can never take it away from you." Clearly he was correct. The fact that Golden Gate University catered to working adults was a perfect match for me, and those of my future students similarly situated and inspired all who participated especially me -Thus when one class I had was in downtown Los Angeles very close to the corner where I used to shine shoes and sell newspapers, as a poor boy, who now lives in one of the

wealthiest parts of California, Newport Beach - where my clients parked their yachts in front of my waterfront office at Lido Marina Village. Even John Wayne's Yacht could be seen from my office. While many of these stars from Orange County have been important, none could ever be truly as great as the iconic actor John Wayne. Born as Marion Morrison, The Duke moved to California from Iowa as a child and was noticed by John Ford when he was working as an assistant on a movie studio. He starred in more than 150 films with many of them directed by Ford. He is an iconic actor who is best known for his roles in western movies like Stagecoach and True Grit. He lived in Newport Harbor in Newport Beach and enjoyed sailing on his old yacht along the shores of the city in Orange County. Today the main Orange County airport is named in honor of John Wayne. A massive bronze sculpture of the him is seen near my office.

I'm now writing this book about my thanks to all who inspired me, including international students, and professors alike- Much more to come later!

Midhurst was wonderful! Quintessential Britain!

Midhurst (/'midh3: rst/) is a market town, parish, and civil parish in West Sussex, England. It lies on the River Rother 20 miles (32 km) inland from the English Channel, and 12 miles (19 km) north of the county town of Chichester. The name Midhurst was first recorded in 1186 as Middeherst, meaning "Middle wooded hill," or "(place) among the wooded hills". It derives from the Old English words midd (adjective) or mid (preposition), meaning "in the middle", plus hyrst, "a wooded hill". The Norman St. Ann's Castle dates from about 1120, although only the foundations are all that can now be seen. The castle, the parish church of St. Mary Magdalene and St. Denis, together with South Pond, the former fish-pond for the castle, are the only three structures left from this early period. The parish church is the oldest building in Midhurst. Just across the River Rother, in the parish of Easebourne, is the ruin of the Tudor Cowdray House. Governance National The former Parliamentary Constituency of Midhurst is now an electoral ward of the Parliamentary Constituency of Chichester, and has been represented in the House of Commons since 2017 by Conservative MP Gillian Keegan.

Welcome to "London Living for Arts and Culture: Exploring Galleries, Theaters, Music Venues, Festivals, and Cultural Events in the City. While there we stayed at a castle where they had horse shows and Jousting. Jousting is when two knights, fully decked out in very heavy armor, charge at each other on horseback with big sticks called lances. And they do it all while trying to hit each other as hard as possible.

My first experience with an English Bobby was when I lived in the wonderful village Hamlet called Conford Park and near West Sussex where my children were going to school in Midhurst. I was walking near the Local church/City Hall, and there were two policemen talking to a man who was a little bit irritated, and he was yelling at them, saying, "You guys don't come when I expect you to come, and when I call you, you're never here," and he was really being aggressive. They were just standing there very quietly listening to him, and finally when he was finished ranting and raving, they said, "Sara, would you, Connie, step into the car," and I thought to myself right then and there after he did step into the car, and they put handcuffs on him. If we were in Los Angeles, he would probably be dead by now. They were very gentlemanly and kind, and the whole episode went away without any incidents. A lovely event in Great Britain. Next time I saw a bar was when I was driving in the Local shopping center, and I was going in there to get some groceries, and as I drove to the parking lot, a policeman pulled up next to me, a Bobby pulled up next to me, and he said, "What are you doing here?" Because I had California license plates on my car, and I said, "I am teaching in London international law," and he just waved his hand and shook his head and left. Those are my first experiences, interestingly enough because I had California license plates, and it was quite a showstopper. My automobile was a Mercedes convertible 550 SL silver, and it was the only one in the city of Midhurst and the only one I saw when I was in London as well so it was a showstopper and I went to pick up my mail at the local mail store shop which is also a mom and Pop grocery store, and I walked in, and I said, "Hi. I'm here to get my mail," and he said, "I said do you want me to show you some identification," he said, "No, I know you are, and I know where you live," so that was really sweet and nice, but clearly demonstrating what happens when you have a California license plate in that part of the world. It was a wonderful experience. Which reminds me of the time I was driving in Switzerland and came upon a 5-way intersection. I saw the police officer on the other side of the intersection and waited for the green light. He stopped me anyway, and I said I saw you there and waited. Come to the other corner, and I will show you! He waved me off and left! My first experience with an English Bobby was when I lived in the wonderful village Hamlet called Comfort Park and near West Sussex where my children were going to school in Midhurst. I was walking near the Local church/City Hall, and there were two policemen talking to a man who was a little bit irritated, and he was yelling at them, saying you guys don't come when I expect you to come and when I call you, you're never here and he was really being aggressive. They were just standing there very quietly listening to him, and finally when he was finished ranting and raving, they said, "Sara, would you, Connie, step into the car," and I thought to myself right then and there after he did step into the car, and they put handcuffs on him. If we were in Los Angeles, he would probably be dead by now. They were very gentlemanly and kind, and the whole episode went away without any incidents. A lovely event in Great Britain. Next time I saw a bar was when I was driving in the Local shopping center, and I was going in there to get some groceries, and as I drove to the parking lot, a policeman pulled up next to me, a Bobby pulled up next to me, and he said, "What are you doing here?" Because I had California license plates on my car, and I said, "I am teaching in London international law," and he just waved his hand and shook his head and left. Those are my first experiences, interestingly enough because I had California license plates, and it was quite a showstopper. My automobile was a Mercedes convertible 550 SL silver, and it was the only one in the city of Midhurst and the only one I saw when I was in London as well so it was a showstopper and I went to pick up my mail at the local mail store shop which is also a mom and Pop grocery store, and I walked in, and I said, "Hi. I'm here to get my mail," and he said, "I said do you want me to show you some identification," he said, "No, I know you are, and I know where you live," so that was really sweet and nice, but clearly demonstrating what happens when you have a California license plate in that part of the world. It was a wonderful experience. Legal systems abroad: Number one England-when I was first in England and rented a car which required you to sit on the other side of the car and shift with your left hand 1 was negotiating a roundabout and a police officer rolled up next to me and said would you please watch your driving mind you're driving it's atrocious.

Number two, when I was in the Netherlands, I was pulled over for no reason at all. The officer came up with a breathalyzer and checked my breath. It happened to be the night of the football playoffs, and I was just returning from the sports club. He said, "Oh, okay, you're fine." I said, "Thank you, everyone else in this country is probably drunk."

Switzerland: I saw a police officer across the intersection, which had several different lines approaching it. I waited patiently until my light turned green. When it did, I proceeded through the intersection, and the police officer came over and pulled me over. He said, "I saw you go through the red light." I said, "No, I did not go through the red light. I looked right at you and I saw you, and I waited until the light was green for me." He just waved his hand and left.

Number four, a police officer in England pulled me over in West Sussex for no reason at all. He said, "What are you doing here?" I said, "I'm teaching international law." He waved his hand and left.

I saw two police officers in the village that I lived in, in West Sussex, talking to a man who was aggravated, walking back and forth, pacing back and forth, and yelling at them, saying, "You never come when I call you." They were about ready to put him under arrest. They were standing very chief page patiently while he was ranting and raving. So, I drove around them, and an hour later when I came back, he was still out of the car. The police were asking very gently, "Would you mind stepping into the car, please?" And he did.

West Sussex is an administrative county of southern England, bordering the English Channel. It lies within the historic county of Sussex, except for a small area in the north around Gatwick Airport, which belongs to the historic county of Surrey. It comprises seven districts: Adur, Arun, Chichester, Horsham, and Mid Sussex, and the boroughs of Crawley and Worthing. The administrative center is Chichester. A ridge of chalk hills, the South Downs, runs across the county from east to west. The northern slopes of the Downs are abrupt, where the chalk gives way to the heavy clays and sands of The Weald. To the south, the Downs slope more gently toward the English Channel. South of Chichester, a fertile coastal plain broadens out into the flat headland of Selsey Bill. Coastal erosion, especially around Selsey Bill, has produced continual changes in the shoreline. Since the beginning of the 19th century, the growth of seaside resorts has been a major factor in the development of the West Sussex coast. Today, the built-up area is almost continuous from Shoreham-by-Sea in the east to Selsey in the west. Littlehampton and Bognor Regis are substantial resorts, and Worthing has developed as a retirement town. Recreational sailing is popular along the indented coastline of the western part of the county. Away from the coast, much of West Sussex remains rural in character, with winding lanes, woodland, and small villages. However, during the 20th century, suburban development spread to the northeastern part of West Sussex, and Gatwick Airport spurred commercial development in and around Crawley. Many residents commute by rail to work in London. The area covers 769 square miles (1,991 square km). The population was 753,614 in 2001 and 806,892 in 2011 preliminaries.

Got in and paid only half price - Loved it!: On

18 April It was announced that Bonnie Langford will join the cast of Chicago as Roxie Hart from Tuesday, 18 April. She will perform through to the last night at the Adelphi Theatre on 22 April and continue when the show transfers to the Cambridge Theatre on 28 April. The show currently stars Linzi Hateley as Roxie Hart (until 17 April), Debbie Kurup as Velma Kelly (until 17 April), Terence Maynard as Billy Flynn until 17 April, while Victor McGuire will continue as Amos Hart into June 2006. Chrissy Hammond and Alex Weatherhill will continue in the roles of Mamma Morton and Mary, respectively, until 17 April. Chicago, which opened at the Adelphi Theatre on 18 November 1997, following previews from 27 October 1997, will end its run at the Adelphi theatre on 22 April 2006. It will then re-open at the Cambridge Theatre on 28 April 2006. The Cambridge Theatre was the London home of Chicago when the first production of the show opened there on 10 April 1979, running for 603 performances. Chicago is based on the play by Maurine Dallas Watkins, has a book by Fred Ebb and Bob Fosse, music by John Kander and lyrics by Fred Ebb. Scenic design is by John Lee Beatty, costume design by William Ivey Long, lighting by Ken Billington and sound by Rick Clarke. Musical supervision is by Rob Fisher, and musical direction is by Gareth Valentine. It is choreographed by Ann Reinking in the style of Bob Fosse and directed by Walter Bobbie.

Great Britain:

To my 007 Auto Friend: We are about 50 min outside of London at the **Cowdray Park Cottages**, near the Polo Grounds. We stayed in the Alps for a year while I taught at the Webster Geneva campus, and that was a blast. Congratulations on your promotion! Way to go, man! We will be in London on the 2nd and 3rd for a weekend get-together with some old friends, and then I have a meeting on the 4th back in London. If you are around, we can have a drink or so after the

Note: Let's start at the beginning. While Bentley may have been the first car driven by James Bond in the novels, **Fleming introduced the Aston Martin DB3 in Goldfinger** following a suggestion from a fan. 007 and Aston Martin have been entwined ever since. In the novels, first released in the early 1950s, Bond drove the Aston Martin DB Mark III. But when it came to the film version of Goldfinger (1964), it was time to use a more contemporary machine. Step forward, the DB5. 4th. Delve Deeper into Britain's Heritage. Immerse yourself in the fascinating history and culture of England, Wales, Scotland or Ireland on a fully escorted, bespoke vacation featuring behind-the-scenes tours and insights from owners of intriguing properties themselves. Travel with experienced Tour Directors, enjoy evening talks from expert guest speakers, stay in well-appointed hotels, discover living examples of Britain's past and indulge in flavorful regional cuisine as specified in each itinerary.

Interesting notes on my Journey from Hollywood to Global MBA students:

1. Hollywood days: Jim Morrison and the doors were headliners at the whiskey go-go in 1966

2. 2003-2004 taught in London, then 2008 Geneva etc.

3. GLOBAL MBA JOKE: Global MBA students, "Does your mother know you smoke? "answer, "the eagle has landed! LOL!

Marylebone Note: I was teaching in London, and there was a great place to shop as I got off the train from West Sussex: **Marylebone**

notable residents: Lord Byron, English romantic poet, born in Marylebone and baptized St Marylebone Parish Church. [38] Charles Dickens, the English writer, lived in 1 Devonshire Terrace, a building that was demolished in the 1950s.[38] Benny Green, an English jazz saxophonist, was born in Marylebone. [39] Robin Hurlstone, the English actor, was born in Marylebone. [40] W. O. G. Lofts, English researcher and author, was born in Marylebone. [41] Paul McCartney, the English musician, wrote "Yesterday" whilst living at 57 Wimpole Street. [42] Norman Wisdom, an English actor, comedian, musician and singer, was born in Marylebone. [43] Transport

Before my marriage to my Dutch wife and after my marriage to my lovely British wife, I was very fortunate to meet lovely ladies from Scandinavia, as mentioned in my previous book, "A Joyful Professor's Global Journey"

I met a lovely lady in Sweden due to the misfortune of a no from my beautiful travel agent in

Lido Marina Village, across from my Law Office on the Bay. When Stacie said no-" lemons to lemonade" this lovely travel agent near my law office at Lido, Marina Village, said she was unable to come with me on my journey and discovery of Scandinavia- You must know that I then noticed that Leningrad was so close to Helsinki Finland, and added that to my trip at last minute! Then, the other important, wonderful, joyful experience that occurred as a result of Stacie's refusal was that I met up with a lovely Swedish medical student while I was in Stockholm. The young, delightful lady was living in a place called Melmo, and she eventually flew into Los Angeles Inter National airport, where I picked her up, and She came to visit me at my place along the Bay and Newport Beach. She stayed for a few days, and it was the beginning of a wonderful friendship and relationship. While in her home country, She also took me on a short tour of Stockholm. And at the time, there was a ferry from Stockholm to her place in Malmo- and we at that time, jumped on the ferry and had a wonderful visit - with a Hometown woman who knew all the delightful places and things to experience. Then, this journey to Scandinavia additionally leads me to a wonderful lady. I met while in Helsinki, Finland this delightful woman came to visit me as well in Newport Beach, and we went swimming on the beach. We went to a wonderful restaurant down in Laguna Beach, and this became another friendship with a lovely lady from that part of the world. The journey, not the destination, is the best!

Malmö is a coastal city in southern Sweden. It lies at the eastern end of the striking Öresund Bridge, a long road and railway bridge-tunnel running to Copenhagen, Denmark. In the city center, Lilla Torg is a cobblestone square with cafes, half-timbered houses and shops selling local handicrafts. Malmö Castle, a 16th-century fortress built by King Christian III of Denmark, houses nature, history and art exhibits. Google

Tower 42 London Near Regents Park London, where I taught school at the university of Regency Park and Webster University. One of my students lived in the home overlooking the Park near the same place where Madonna owned a home. Regent's Park (officially The Regent's Park) is one of the Royal Parks of London. It occupies high ground in north-west Inner London, administratively split between the City of Westminster and the Borough of Camden (and historically between Marylebone and Saint Pancras parishes).[1] It contains Regent's University and London Zoo. This was all near the Sherlock Holmes Museum in London.

Loved leading this class on CROSSROADS OF EUROPE (Private) 9 days

DAYS 1-2: ARRIVAL A dream comes true as you board an international flight headed for Europe. Scarcely a wink and a movie later, you're in London, the hub and focus for theatergoers worldwide. Settle into your hotel, then set out to explore your surroundings. Red, double-decker buses groan along the 'wrong' side of the road, escorted by innumerable black taxicabs with engines that sound like sewing machines. The adventure begins! Try out the Tube or take a ride on a double-decker bus! Explore the city's shopping areas, including Piccadilly and Knightsbridge. Don't miss Harrods, the world-famous department store. Dinner and overnight in London. DAY 3: LONDON CITY SIGHTSEEING A professional guide accompanies you this morning on a tour of the sights and sounds of the British capital. See Westminster Abbey, the Houses of Parliament, Big Ben, Trafalgar Square, St. Paul's, Soho, Oxford Street, 10 Downing Street and the Changing of the Guard at Buckingham Palace if it is scheduled today. This afternoon is free to arrange as you wish. Consider a visit to the Tower of London to view the Traitors' Gate, the Bloody Tower, the Block (where two of Henry VIII's ill-fated wives lost their heads), the White Tower and the Crown Jewels. If you choose to follow one of the Beefeaters, you'll also be able to visit the Royal Chapel. The London theatre scene is unmatched in Europe, from classical drama to Shakespeare, from whodunits to musicals. Tonight, consider a West End theatre performance. Dinner and overnight in London.

DAY 4: CHUNNEL TRAIN TO BRUSSELS, DRIVE-THROUGH TOUR, BRUGES WALKING TOUR This morning, board the high-speed Eurostar train for the

short trip under the English Channel, arriving less than three hours later in Brussels, the capital of Belgium, and headquarters for NATO and the European Union. Discover this cosmopolitan city on a drive-through tour: see landmarks such as the Royal Palace and the Grand Place, the heart of the Old Town, with the Gothic Town Hall. Of course, you will also see the well-known Manneken-pis fountain! Continue to Bruges, once a modest fortification against Norman invaders, later a world-famous trading center and cradle of Flemish art, now a beautiful reminder of medieval times and pageantry. With your courier, stroll through this city, which values its traditions and radiates charm, and has been dubbed as 'the most medieval town in Europe.' You'll see the Markt (market square), the Basilica of the Holy Blood and the ornate City Hall. This evening, you may want to go to Rozenhoedkaii, from which you can catch the best of all the distractingly beautiful views of Bruges, or to the Huidenvettersplein, a small square filled with café terraces, popular with street artists. Dinner and overnight in Bruges. DAY 5: DELTA EXPO, POLDER LANDS, KINDERDIJK, AMSTERDAM Today's itinerary is one of the most extraordinary in Europe. Enjoy the unique landscape as your coach travels through polder lands and the vast delta of the Rhine River and Schelde River, one arm of which you'll cross using the Westerschelde Tunnel. Continue through polder lands to the massive Storm Barrier, an engineering feat designed to protect low-lying regions. There, you will learn how Holland defends itself against the encroaching sea on a visit to the Delta Expo. No trip to Holland would be complete without a glimpse of majestic windmills with their sails turning gracefully above an. The endless expanse of canals, dikes and polder lands. The finest collection of windmills is to be found at Kinderdijk, now a UNESCO World heritage site, where you'll see the oldest working wooden windmills in the country, still draining the surrounding fields. Continue north to the nominal capital city of the Netherlands, Amsterdam, where the evening is free to spend as you wish. Dinner and overnight in Amsterdam. DAY 6: AMSTERDAM CITY SIGHTSEEING, CANAL CRUISE This morning includes city sightseeing of Amsterdam, old and new, with a local guide.

Loved my polo time in West Sussex!

See 17th- and 18th-century patrician houses and historic landmarks, including the Oudekerk (Old

Church), Nieuwekerk (New Church) and the Westerkerk (West Church), where Rembrandt is buried. Visits are included to a diamond-cutting workshop and to the house, which was the hiding place of the Frank family for two years before they were deported to Germany by the Nazis. The rooms described by Anne Frank in her journal have been preserved as they were when she lived there. Anne began her life in hiding when she turned 14 and died in a concentration camp at the age of 16. This afternoon, enjoy the sightseeing of your choice in the city or consider an optional excursion to the Old World village of Zaanse Schans, where you'll see the manufacture of Dutch cheese and wooden shoes. The excursion also includes a visit to the enchanting fishing village of Volendam. In this simple hamlet, you'll see a traditional harbor of fishing boats with brown sails, little houses with painted wooden façades, women washing thresholds and men walking to work in their wide, baggy trousers, carrying casks of smoked eels. (Remember Hans Brinker?) Return to Amsterdam. Did you know that this 'Venice of the North' is composed of some 90 islands connected by about 1,000 bridges? See for yourself during a cruise on the city's canals. Dinner and overnight in Amsterdam. DAY 7: THALYS TRAIN TO PARIS, CITY SIGHTSEEING Exciting time this morning as you board the high-speed Thalys train for the journey to France. Time flies aboard the streamlined cars, which, inside, look and feel like an airplane. Arrive in the Gare du Nord in downtown Paris, the City of Light! This afternoon, enjoy a coach tour of the city in the company of a local guide. On the Right Bank of the River Seine, see the Champs-Elysées, Napoléon's Arc de Triomphe and the exuberant Opéra Garnier. On the Left Bank, discover the Eiffel Tower, the Invalides, the Latin Quarter and Saint-Germain-des-Prés. Standing proudly on an island in the midst of all this glory is Paris' jewel, Notre-Dame Cathedral. This evening, you may want to head for Montmartre, Paris' highest hill and its most celebrated bohemian district. Artists still flock to the charming Place du Tertre, as they did when Toulouse-Lautrec painted the French Cancan dancers at the famous Moulin Rouge. Enjoy panoramic views of the city as you make your way to the Sacré-Coeur, the white-domed basilica that anchors the Parisian skyline. Dinner and overnight in Paris.

DAY 8: LOUVRE, NOTRE-DAME, BATEAUX-MOUCHES, ILLUMINATIONS This morning, visit the Louvre. Explore its newly-opened galleries and their ancient treasures, as well as the modernistic underground galleria beneath me. M. Pei's glass pyramid. You'll see Leonardo da Vinci's Mona Lisa and the Vénus de Milo, among countless other masterpieces. Plan to have lunch at the Galeries Lafayette, the most elegant of the city's department stores with its splendid 19th-century glass and iron atrium. The cafeteria is located on the 6th floor, from which there's an extraordinary rooftop view of Paris, with the fabulous gilded roof of the Opéra Garnier in the forefront. You may want to stroll through the shopping district around the Opéra. This afternoon, make your way to the Ile de la Cité, the very heart of the ancient city which the Romans called Lutetia, for a visit to Notre-Dame. This cathedral has presided over centuries of glorious and somber French history, from its construction in the Middle Ages to the French Revolution and the coronation of Napoléon in 1804 (the 35-year-old upstart crowned himself emperor)! Admire the bas-reliefs, statuary, gargoyles and remarkable rose windows. While in the area, consider a visit to the former Royal Chapel known as the Sainte-Chapelle, a true gem commissioned by Louis IX in the 13th century to house relics brought back from the crusades, in particular Christ's Sacred Crown of Thorns. The sanctuary combines superb acoustics, soaring architecture and a visual symphony of brilliant colors when sunlight pours in through its magnificent stained-glass windows. For Da Vinci Code thrills, you may prefer to visit the church of Saint-Sulpice, which is known for its impressive interior decoration, in particular the chapels with murals painted by the 19th-century Romantic artist Delacroix. The church is more famous nowadays for its gnomon (obelisk) that was installed by astronomers in 1743, along with the brass line inserted in the stone pavement.

This evening, see Paris transformed into a wonderland like no other during a Bateaux-Mouchescruise along the River Seine, followed by an illumination drive past the most famous monuments of the French capital. Dinner and overnight in Paris. DAY 9: RETURN FLIGHT Most good things must come to an end. Your suitcase full of memorabilia and photos is ready to be processed, you'll arrive home later today, eager to share your discoveries with family and friends. INCLUDES Round-trip transatlantic transportation on scheduled airlines.

• Airport and train station transfers. Accommodations in centrally-located three-star or four- star hotels. Services of a specially-trained passport courier throughout. Deluxe motorcoach, with driver, per itinerary. HIGHLIGHTS Professionally-guided coach tour of London. Chunnel

crossing on the Eurostar train London-Brussels. Drive-through tour of Brussels. Walking tour in Bruges. Polder lands, including the Westerschelde Tunnel, a visit to Delta Expo, and the windmills of Kinderdijk. Professionally-guided coach tour of Amsterdam, including visits to Anne Frank's House and a diamond-cutting workshop. Amsterdam canal cruise. High-speed THALYS train Amsterdam-Paris. Professionally-guided coach tour of Paris. Visit to the Louvre Museum. Visit to Notre-Dame. Bateaux-Mouches cruise and illumination drive. OVERNIGHTS London - 2 nights Bruges 1 night Amsterdam 2 nights Paris - 2 nights. All breakfasts and dinners are included. NOTE: Lifetime membership valid for unlimited travel with passports. All original material copyright© Passports, Inc., 1993-2004. All rights reserved. More new features than ever.

Tate Modern: Explore modern and contemporary art from around the world. See some of the world's most exciting modern and contemporary art at Tate Modern. Enjoy innovative works that shaped art as we know it. Our gallery is free to visit, and on display are paintings, sculptures and large-scale installations from artists around the world, including Pablo Picasso, Yayoi Kusama and Henri Matisse. Explore the iconic Turbine Hall alongside our underground Tanks, a striking space dedicated to live performances and video. Members enjoy unlimited free entry to exhibitions with no need to book. Yayoi Kusama: Infinity Mirror Rooms, however, still requires a free Member ticket, given the show's special and intimate scale. Find out what changes we've made to keep you safe.

-In Closing

The importance of education can never be overestimated. They say that "to teach is to change lives forever." Yet of most importance is that if you look around at all the people in the world that you come in contact with, they are all teachers in one way or another! From the "essential workers" who sacrifice so much, especially during the recent pandemic, such as the hospital workers, the pharmacy workers, the supermarket workers, and teachers, as well as all those who kept education at the forefront of lives by providing books at the local bookstore and help when someone was looking for what they needed to complete their lives. We all can learn much by just observing and realizing that these wonderful men and women are changing lives on a daily basis. In ways that can "Never be taken away!" One of the ways I frequently started my classes was by asking the following question: "If you had unlimited resources and money were no object, what would you do with your life?" Many of my students would answer that they would travel And see the world.

The most important "icing on the cake" of my entire teaching experience was the creation of a course called "Comparative United States - European Union Law." This was the course where I traveled with my students from London to Brussels, Bruges, Amsterdam and Paris - and then again From Venice to Nice, Monte Carlo, to Florence and Rome - And then back to Venice! And in doing so, my hope and prayer is it this education, which can "never be taken away," did indeed change the lives of my students! And that this life experience was an education for me and all the students I came in contact with that can, in closing, "never be taken away," to use the words of my Father when I was a young child selling newspapers on the corner and shining shoes. With Heartfelt thanks, gratitude and love to all the teachers in my life, starting with my parents, family members, and school teachers that I learned my entire life, I devote this work and recollection of my global journey as evidence that teachers in every way, changed my life forever. God Bless!

This book is designed to be a comprehensive guide for students and parents who are interested in immersing themselves in the vibrant arts and culture scene that London has to offer.

Whether you are a family looking for family-friendly activities or an art enthusiast searching for the best galleries and theaters, this book has you covered. Although the Park was initially the idea of Prince Regent George IV and was named for him, [6] James Burton, the pre-eminent London property developer, was responsible for the social and financial patronage of the majority of John Nash's London designs, [7] and for their construction.[8] Architectural scholar Guy Williams has written, "John Nash relied on James Burton for moral and financial support in his great enterprises. Decimus had shown precocious talent as a draughtsman and as an exponent of the classical style... John Nash needed the son's aid, as well as the Father's". [7]Subsequent to the Crown Estate's refusal to finance them, James Burton agreed to personally finance the construction projects of John Nash at Regent's Park, which he had already been commissioned to construct:[9][8] consequently, in 1816, Burton purchased many of the leases of the proposed terraces around, and proposed villas within Regent's Park,[9] and, in 1817, Burton purchased the leases of five of the largest blocks on Regent Street. [9] The first property to be constructed in or around Regent's Park by Burton was his own mansion, The Holme, which was designed by his son, Decimus Burton, and completed in 1818. [9] Burton's extensive financial involvement "effectively guaranteed the success of the project."[9] In return, Nash agreed to promote the career of Decimus Burton. [9] Such were James Burton's contributions to the project that the Commissioners of Woods described James, not Nash, as "the architect of Regent's Park".[10]

Section 1: London Living for Families

- Emphasize family-friendly neighborhoods in London, with recommendations for suitable areas to live for families.

Discuss the best schools in London, focusing on those that offer arts and cultural programs for students.

- Explore the various parks and green spaces in London, highlighting their suitability for children and families.

- Provide a list of activities and attractions suitable for children in London, such as museums, interactive exhibits, and family-friendly festivals.

Section 2: London Living for Arts and Culture

Focus on the rich art scene in London, providing an overview of the top art galleries and museums in the city.

Highlight the renowned theaters in London, discussing the best venues for theater performances and musicals.

Explore the diverse music scene in London, featuring iconic music venues and festivals that showcase a wide range of genres.

Provide a comprehensive calendar of cultural events happening in London throughout the year, including festivals, exhibitions, and performances.

Conclusion:

- "London Living for Arts and Culture: Exploring Galleries, Theaters, Music Venues, Festivals, and Cultural Events in the City" is a must-have guide for students and parents looking to make the most of London's vibrant arts and culture scene.
- With recommendations for family-friendly neighborhoods, schools with arts programs, and a comprehensive list of galleries, theaters, music venues, festivals, and cultural events, this book is your ultimate resource for London living.
- Get ready to immerse yourself in the rich arts and culture of London and create unforgettable memories in this vibrant city.

Audience: Students and Parents

London Living for Arts and Culture: Exploring Galleries, Theaters, Music Venues, Festivals, and Cultural Events in the City

Welcome to "London Living for Arts and Culture: Exploring Galleries, Theaters, Music Venues, Festivals, and Cultural Events in the City!" This subchapter is specifically tailored to our audience of students and parents, encompassing the niches of London Living for Families and London Living for Arts and Culture. Here, we will delve into the vibrant art scene of London while also offering insights into family-friendly neighborhoods, schools, parks, and activities suitable for children in the city.

For students and parents seeking to immerse themselves in the arts and culture of London, this book is your ultimate guide. London is renowned for its world-class galleries, theaters, music venues, festivals, and cultural events, and we are here to help you navigate through this vibrant tapestry.

Students, whether you are pursuing your studies in arts or simply have a passion for creativity, London is the place to be. This city is teeming with opportunities for aspiring artists, actors, musicians, and dancers. Discover the iconic art galleries such as Tate Modern, National Gallery, and Saatchi Gallery, where you can marvel at masterpieces from renowned artists. Attend captivating theater performances in the West End or explore the alternative theater scene in Camden or Shoreditch. Get your groove on at music venues like the O2 Arena, the Royal Albert Hall, or intimate jazz clubs scattered throughout the city. And let's not forget the countless festivals and cultural events happening all year round, from Notting Hill Carnival to the vibrant celebrations during Chinese New Year.

For parents, we understand that your priority is finding family-friendly neighborhoods, schools, parks, and activities for your children. London offers a plethora of options that cater to families. Explore neighborhoods like Richmond, Hampstead, or Greenwich, known for their excellent schools, safe environment, and proximity to parks and green spaces. Take your little ones to the London Zoo, the Natural History Museum, or the Science Museum, where they can learn while having fun. Enjoy picnics in Hyde Park, boat rides along the Thames, or cycling in Victoria Park.

Whether you are a parent looking for family-friendly activities or a student eager to explore the arts and culture of London, this subchapter has something for everyone. Prepare to be inspired, entertained, and captivated by the magic that London has to offer. Let the journey begin!

Chapter 1: Introduction to London Living for Arts and Culture

The Vibrant Arts and Culture Scene in London

London has long been known as a global hub for arts and culture, attracting artists, performers, and creatives from all corners of the world. From its iconic theaters and art galleries to its vibrant music venues and lively festivals, the city offers a rich tapestry of cultural experiences for students and parents alike.

Art Galleries: London is home to some of the world's most renowned art galleries, showcasing a diverse range of artistic styles and movements. The Tate Modern, located on the banks of the River Thames, is a must-visit for art enthusiasts, housing an extensive collection of modern and contemporary art. The National Gallery and the Victoria and Albert Museum are also popular destinations, offering an array of classical and historical artworks.

Theaters: London's West End is synonymous with world-class theater productions, including long-running musicals, dramas, and comedies. From iconic venues such as the Royal Opera House and the Royal Albert Hall to the smaller, independent theaters scattered throughout the city, there is always a captivating performance to be enjoyed. Students and parents can immerse themselves in the magic of live theater and witness some of the best talent the world has to offer.

Music Venues: For music lovers, London is a treasure trove of venues catering to all tastes and genres. Whether it's catching a live gig at the O2 Arena, experiencing the intimate atmosphere of the Jazz Cafe, or exploring the underground music scene in venues like the Camden Assembly, there is something for everyone. Students and parents can discover new bands, support emerging artists, or simply enjoy a night of live music in this vibrant city.

Festivals and Cultural Events:

London truly comes alive during its numerous festivals and cultural events that take place throughout the year. The Notting Hill Carnival, held annually in August, is a vibrant celebration of Caribbean culture featuring colorful parades, live music, and delicious food. The Southbank Centre hosts a variety of festivals, including the London Literature Festival and the Women of the World Festival, promoting diversity and inclusivity. Students and parents can immerse themselves in these cultural celebrations and experience the city's diverse heritage.

In conclusion, London's arts and culture scene offers a wealth of opportunities for students and parents to explore and engage with. From the city's world-class art galleries and theaters to its diverse music venues and exciting festivals, there is always something new and exciting happening in this vibrant city. Whether you're a family looking for family-friendly activities or an art and culture enthusiast seeking inspiration, London is sure to captivate and inspire.

Chapter 2: Exploring Art Galleries in London

World-Renowned Art Galleries in the City

London is a city that thrives on art and culture, and its world-renowned art galleries are a testament to this fact. Whether you are a student looking to explore the art scene or a parent wanting to expose your children to the wonders of artistic expression, London has something for everyone. In this subchapter, we will delve into the top art galleries in the city that are a must-visit for both students and parents.

The National Gallery, located in Trafalgar Square, is a true gem of the art world. With over 2,300 paintings from the 13th to the 19th centuries, it houses masterpieces by renowned artists such as Van Gogh, Monet, and Da Vinci. The gallery offers free admission, making it an ideal destination for students on a tight budget. It also hosts regular workshops and events for children, making it an educational and enjoyable experience for the whole family.

Another iconic gallery is the Tate Modern, situated on the banks of the River Thames. It is the world's most visited modern art gallery, featuring works by contemporary artists like Picasso, Warhol, and Hockney. The gallery offers guided tours and interactive exhibits for children, encouraging their creativity and imagination. Parents can also enjoy the stunning views of London from the Tate Modern's viewing platform while their children explore the art installations.

For those interested in contemporary art, the Saatchi Gallery is a must-visit. Located in Chelsea, it showcases the work of emerging artists from around the world. The gallery regularly hosts family-friendly events, including art workshops and storytelling sessions, making it a great choice for parents looking to introduce their children to the world of contemporary art.

If you are a student or parent looking for a more immersive art experience, the Victoria and Albert

Museum is the perfect choice. It is the world's largest museum of art and design, housing a vast collection that spans over 5,000 years of human creativity. The museum offers educational programs for students and families, including hands-on workshops and interactive exhibits.

London's art galleries are not just a feast for the eyes but also an opportunity to learn, explore, and be inspired. Whether you are a student seeking inspiration for your own artistic endeavors or a parent wanting to foster a love for art in your children, these world-renowned galleries are the perfect destination. So, grab your sketchbook, bring your family along, and immerse yourself in the vibrant art scene that London has to offer.

Must-Visit Contemporary Art Galleries in London

London is a vibrant hub for art and culture, and its contemporary art scene is no exception. For students and parents seeking to immerse themselves in the thriving art world of the city, there are several must-visit contemporary art galleries that offer a unique and enriching experience. In this subchapter, we will explore some of the top contemporary art galleries in London, catering to both students and families.

1. Tate Modern: Located on the South Bank of the River Thames, Tate Modern is one of the world's most renowned contemporary art museums. It houses an impressive collection of contemporary artworks from artists around the globe. With its vast exhibition spaces and interactive displays, Tate Modern offers a captivating experience for art enthusiasts of all ages.

2. Saatchi Gallery: Situated in the heart of Chelsea, the Saatchi Gallery showcases exciting and thought-provoking contemporary art from emerging artists. Its dynamic exhibitions and installations provide a platform for young talents and offer a fresh perspective on the art world.

3. Whitechapel Gallery: Known for its commitment to showcasing innovative and experimental

contemporary art, the Whitechapel Gallery is a must-visit for those seeking cutting-edge artworks. Its diverse program includes exhibitions, talks, and screenings that encourage dialogue and engagement with contemporary art.

4. Serpentine Galleries: Comprising two galleries, the Serpentine Gallery and the Serpentine Sackler Gallery, this institution is renowned for its temporary exhibitions featuring contemporary artists. The Serpentine Galleries also hosts the annual Serpentine Pavilion, a unique architectural installation that attracts visitors from all over the world.

5. The Barbican Centre: Beyond being a world-class performing arts venue, the Barbican Centre houses a remarkable art gallery. With its eclectic mix of contemporary art exhibitions, film screenings, and live performances, it offers a truly immersive experience for art and culture enthusiasts.

6. Victoria Miro: Situated in Mayfair and Venice, Victoria Miro Gallery showcases a diverse range of contemporary art, including paintings, sculptures, and installations. It represents both established and emerging artists, making it an exciting space for discovering new talent.

Visiting these contemporary art galleries in London will not only expose students and parents to the latest trends in contemporary art but also provide a platform for dialogue, inspiration, and cultural enrichment. Whether you are a seasoned art lover or just starting to explore the art world, these galleries offer something for everyone, making them an essential part of any visit to London.

Hidden Gems: Lesser-Known Art Galleries in London

London is renowned for its thriving arts and culture scene, with a plethora of world-class museums and galleries that attract visitors from all over the globe. While iconic institutions like the Tate Modern and the National Gallery often steal the limelight, there are numerous lesser- known art galleries in the city that offer a unique and intimate experience for art enthusiasts. In this subchapter, we will explore some of London's hidden gems, perfect for students and parents looking to discover a more offbeat side of the city's art scene.

One such hidden gem is the Dulwich Picture Gallery, located in the leafy suburb of Dulwich. Established in 1811, this gallery houses an impressive collection of European old masters, including works by Rembrandt, Van Dyck, and Poussin. The gallery's peaceful surroundings and charming architecture make it an ideal destination for families seeking a tranquil art experience away from the hustle and bustle of central London.

Another hidden gem is the White Cube Bermondsey, situated in a former warehouse in Southwark. This contemporary art gallery showcases cutting-edge works by renowned artists such as Tracey Emin and Damien Hirst. With its vast exhibition spaces and innovative installations, the White Cube Bermondsey offers a thought-provoking and immersive experience for both students and parents.

For those interested in modern and contemporary art, the Camden Arts Centre is not to be missed. Tucked away in the vibrant neighborhood of Camden, this gallery hosts temporary exhibitions featuring emerging artists alongside well-established names. The center also offers a range of educational programs and workshops for children, making it an excellent choice for families looking to engage their little ones in the world of art.

If you're seeking something truly unconventional, the Viktor Wynd Museum of Curiosities, Fine Art & Natural History is sure to captivate your imagination. Located in Hackney, this eccentric gallery houses a bizarre collection of oddities, including taxidermy animals, ancient artifacts, and peculiar artworks. A visit to this quirky museum is a truly unique experience that will leave both parents and children intrigued and inspired.

London's art scene is not limited to the well-known galleries; there are hidden gems waiting to be discovered by students and parents alike. Whether you're seeking classical masterpieces, contemporary installations, or offbeat curiosities, these lesser-known art galleries offer a diverse and enriching cultural experience for the whole family. So why not venture off the beaten path and explore the hidden treasures that London has to offer?

Chapter 3: Unveiling London's Theatrical Wonders

Historic Theaters and Their Rich Performances

London is not only a city of modern architectural marvels and bustling streets, but it is also a city steeped in history and culture. One aspect of this cultural heritage can be found in its historic theaters, which have witnessed countless memorable performances throughout the years. In this subchapter, we will delve into the fascinating world of London's historic theaters and explore the rich performances that have graced their stages.

London's historic theaters are not merely architectural wonders; they are living symbols of the city's artistic legacy. These theaters have stood the test of time, with some dating back several centuries. Their ornate interiors, with plush velvet seats, grand chandeliers, and exquisite detailing, transport audiences to a bygone era of elegance and sophistication.

One such iconic theater is the Royal Opera House, located in Covent Garden. This majestic venue has been a hub for world-class opera and ballet performances since its opening in 1732. From the mesmerizing melodies of Mozart and Verdi to the graceful movements of legendary ballet dancers, the Royal Opera House has witnessed countless historic performances that have left audiences in awe.

Another historic gem is the Globe Theatre, a faithful reconstruction of the original theater where renowned playwright William Shakespeare's plays were first performed. Stepping into the globe is like stepping back in time, as actors in authentic costumes bring Shakespeare's timeless works to life in the open-air setting. It is a truly immersive experience that allows audiences to connect with the past and appreciate the enduring genius of the Bard.

The Theatre Royal Drury Lane is yet another historic theater with a storied past. Established in 1663, it has been home to countless groundbreaking performances, including musicals, comedies, and dramas. From the haunting melodies of Andrew Lloyd Webber's "The Phantom of the Opera" to the uproarious laughter of Oscar Wilde's "The Importance of Being Earnest," the Theatre Royal Drury Lane has been a stage for some of the most memorable productions in London's theater history.

For students and parents seeking a cultural experience that combines entertainment and education, London's historic theaters offer a unique opportunity. Many of these theaters organize special performances and workshops tailored to young audiences, making them an Ideal destination for families. From interactive children's plays to behind-the-scenes tours, these theaters provide an enriching experience that sparks creativity and fosters a lifelong love for the arts.

In conclusion, London's historic theaters are not only architectural marvels but also guardians of the city's artistic heritage. They have witnessed countless performances that have left an indelible mark on the cultural landscape of the city. For students and parents, exploring these theaters is an opportunity to immerse oneself in the rich history and vibrant performances that continue to captivate audiences today. Whether you are a theater enthusiast or simply seeking a family-friendly cultural experience, London's historic theaters are a must-visit destination.

Contemporary Theaters and Cutting-Edge Productions

London is renowned for its thriving arts and culture scene, and nowhere is this more evident than in its contemporary theaters and cutting-edge productions. This subchapter explores the exciting world of modern theater in the city, providing a glimpse into the diverse and innovative performances that await both students and parents.

London's contemporary theaters are at the forefront of pushing boundaries and challenging traditional theatrical conventions. Productions in these venues often feature experimental staging techniques, thought-provoking narratives, and avant-garde performances that push the limits of what is possible on stage. From immersive theater experiences to interactive performances, audiences are invited to become active participants in the storytelling process.

One of the most iconic contemporary theater venues in London is the National Theatre. Located on the South Bank, it showcases a wide range of cutting-edge productions from both established and emerging playwrights. With its state-of-the-art facilities and commitment to artistic excellence, the National Theatre is a must-visit destination for theater enthusiasts.

Another notable venue is the Royal Court Theatre, renowned for its dedication to supporting new and emerging playwrights. It is a hotbed of creativity, often showcasing bold and thought-provoking works that tackle contemporary social and political issues. Attending a play at the Royal Court Theatre is not only an opportunity to witness groundbreaking performances but also a chance to engage in conversations that matter.

For families interested in exposing their children to the world of theater, the Unicorn Theatre is a fantastic choice. As the UK's leading theater for young audiences, it offers a diverse program of performances suitable for children of all ages. From imaginative adaptations of classic fairy tales to interactive workshops that encourage creativity and self-expression, the Unicorn Theatre provides an enriching experience for the whole family.

London's contemporary theaters and cutting-edge productions are an integral part of the city's vibrant arts and culture scene. By immersing themselves in these innovative performances, students and parents can gain a deeper appreciation for the power of theater as a medium for storytelling and social commentary. Whether you're a theater enthusiast or a family looking for an enriching cultural experience, London's contemporary theaters are sure to captivate and inspire.

West End Shows and the Spectacle of Musical Theater

London's West End is renowned worldwide for its spectacular array of musical theater productions. From iconic classics to contemporary hits, the West End offers a thrilling and unforgettable experience for students and parents alike. In this subchapter, we delve into the magic of West End shows and explore how they contribute to the cultural tapestry of the city.

The West End is home to some of the most famous and beloved musicals in history. From the timeless beauty of "The Phantom of the Opera" to the high-energy extravaganza of "Mamma Mia!", there is something for everyone's taste. These shows not only entertain but also educate and inspire, making them an ideal choice for family outings.

Attending a West End show is a truly immersive experience. The grand theaters, with their ornate architecture and plush interiors, transport you to a world of elegance and glamour. The elaborate set designs, dazzling costumes, and stunning special effects create a visual spectacle that captivates the audience from start to finish. The performances, delivered by incredibly talented actors and singers, are nothing short of awe-inspiring.

For students, West End shows provide a unique opportunity to appreciate the performing arts and witness firsthand the dedication and skill required to put on such a production. They can gain a deeper understanding of different art forms, from acting to choreography, and develop an appreciation for the hard work and creativity that goes into making a musical come alive on stage.

Parents, on the other hand, can relish the joy of sharing these magical moments with their children. Watching their little ones' faces light up as they witness the magic unfold before their eyes is truly priceless. The West End offers a range of family-friendly shows with themes and storylines that resonate with audiences of all ages. It's a chance for families to come together and create lifelong memories.

London's West End shows are not just entertainment; they are a celebration of the city's rich cultural heritage. They showcase the diversity and talent that thrives within the theater community and contribute to London's reputation as a global hub for arts and culture. So, whether you're a student looking for an educational experience or a parent seeking a memorable family outing, make sure to catch a West End show and immerse yourself in the spectacle of musical theater.

Chapter 4: Immersing in London's Music Venues

Legendary Music Venues in London

London has a rich history of music and is home to some of the most iconic and legendary music venues in the world. Whether you are a music enthusiast or just looking to experience the vibrant music scene in the city, these venues offer a range of genres and unforgettable performances. In this subchapter, we will explore some of the must-visit music venues that have shaped London's music culture.

1. The O2 Arena: This massive arena has hosted some of the biggest names in the music industry, from Beyoncé to The Rolling Stones. With a capacity of over 20,000, it is the go-to venue for large-scale concerts and events. The O2 Arena also houses smaller venues, such as Indigo and Brooklyn Bowl, offering a diverse range of music experiences.

2. The Royal Albert Hall: A true architectural gem, The Royal Albert Hall is renowned for its stunning circular design and incredible acoustics. It has hosted countless iconic performances, including classical concerts, rock gigs, and the annual BBC Proms. Attending a concert here is a truly magical experience.

3. Camden Roundhouse: Located in the vibrant Camden Town, Camden Roundhouse is a historic venue that has seen performances by legendary artists like Jimi Hendrix and Pink Floyd. The venue's unique circular shape and intimate setting create an immersive experience for concert-goers.

4. Brixton Academy: Known for its electric atmosphere, Brixton Academy has been a prominent venue for rock, indie, and alternative music. The venue has played host to bands like The Clash and The Prodigy, and its iconic stage and balcony make for an unforgettable live music experience.

5. Ronnie Scott's Jazz Club: For jazz enthusiasts, Ronnie Scott's is a must-visit venue. Located in the heart of Soho, this intimate club has been a hub for jazz legends since 1959. From traditional jazz to contemporary fusion, Ronnie Scott showcases the finest talent in the genre.

6. The Jazz Café: Another iconic venue for jazz, soul, and world music is The Jazz Café in Camden. This intimate venue hosts both established artists and emerging talents, providing an up-close and personal experience for music lovers.

London's legendary music venues offer an array of experiences for students and parents alike. Whether you're seeking a night of rock, jazz, or classical music, these venues provide a platform for some of the most talented artists in the world. With their rich history and vibrant atmospheres, these venues are sure to leave a lasting impression on anyone looking to immerse themselves in London's thriving music scene.

Live Music Scene: From Jazz to Indie

London is renowned for its vibrant and diverse live music scene, offering a rich tapestry of genres to suit all tastes. From the smooth melodies of jazz to the raw energy of indie rock, the city is a haven for music lovers of all ages. In this subchapter, we will explore the various facets of London's live music scene, showcasing the incredible range of talent and venues that make the city a hub for musical innovation and creativity.

Jazz enthusiasts will be delighted to discover a plethora of venues dedicated to this timeless genre. From iconic establishments like Ronnie Scott's, where legends such as Ella Fitzgerald and Miles Davis have graced the stage, to intimate jazz clubs like Kansas Smitty's, London offers a myriad of options to experience the magic of improvisation and soulful melodies.

For those with a penchant for the alternative, London's indie music scene is thriving. From established venues such as Camden's Roundhouse to underground haunts like The Windmill in Brixton, there is an abundance of spaces for up-and-coming bands to showcase their talent. The city's indie scene is known for its unique blend of genres, with influences ranging from punk and garage rock to dream pop and folk.

Parents and students alike will be pleased to know that London's live music scene caters to all ages and interests. Many venues offer family-friendly events, ensuring that even the youngest music enthusiasts can enjoy the magic of a live performance. From interactive concerts for children to outdoor festivals showcasing diverse musical acts, there are numerous opportunities for families to bond over the power of music.

London's live music scene is not limited to traditional venues. The city also boasts a vibrant street performance culture, with talented buskers lining the bustling streets of Covent Garden, Southbank, and Camden Market. These impromptu performances add a touch of spontaneity and charm to the city's already vibrant atmosphere, providing a unique and memorable experience for both locals and tourists.

Whether you are a jazz aficionado, an indie music enthusiast, or simply appreciate the joy of live performances, London's music scene offers something for everyone. From iconic jazz clubs to intimate indie venues, the city's diverse range of musical offerings ensures that there is never a dull moment for those seeking to immerse themselves in the magic of live music. So grab your friends and family, and prepare to be swept away by the captivating rhythms and melodies that define London's live music scene.

Intimate Venues for Acoustic Performances and Emerging Artists

For students and parents looking to immerse themselves in the vibrant arts and culture scene of London, there is no shortage of opportunities to explore. One aspect of this rich tapestry is the thriving world of intimate venues for acoustic performances and emerging artists. These hidden gems provide a unique and personal experience, allowing audiences to connect with the music on a deeper level.

London is home to a multitude of intimate venues scattered throughout the city, each with its own distinct character. From cozy cafes to underground bars, these spaces offer an intimate setting where budding musicians can showcase their talents and establish themselves in the industry. For parents seeking to expose their children to the wonders of live music, these venues provide an ideal environment that is both safe and engaging.

One such venue is The Troubadour, located in the heart of Earls Court. This iconic establishment has been hosting acoustic performances since the 1950s and has become a breeding ground for emerging talent. With its intimate atmosphere and close proximity to several schools and parks, The Troubadour is a perfect destination for families looking to enjoy an evening of live music together.

Another must-visit venue is The Green Note in Camden. This cozy basement bar is renowned for its support of emerging artists and its commitment to acoustic music. With its rustic charm and an eclectic lineup of performances, The Green Note provides a truly immersive experience for music lovers of all ages.

For those seeking a more alternative vibe, the Bush Hall in Shepherd's Bush is a hidden gem worth discovering. This beautifully restored Edwardian dance hall offers an intimate setting for acoustic performances, making it an ideal venue for families to enjoy an evening of music and culture.

Whether you are a student looking to explore London's diverse music scene or a parent wanting to share the joy of live music with your children, the city has a plethora of intimate venues to suit your needs. These spaces not only provide an opportunity to experience emerging artists up close but also offer a welcoming environment for families to come together and create lasting memories.

So, why not venture out and discover the enchanting world of intimate venues for acoustic performances and emerging artists? London's thriving arts and culture scene awaits, ready to captivate both students and parents alike.

Chapter 5: Celebrating Festivals in London

Traditional Festivals Rooted in London's Culture and History

London is a city rich in culture and history, and its traditional festivals are a testament to its vibrant past. These festivals not only celebrate the city's heritage but also provide a unique opportunity for students and parents to immerse themselves in the local traditions and experience the true essence of London living.

One such festival is the Notting Hill Carnival, held annually in August. This colorful and lively event is a celebration of Caribbean culture and is the largest street festival in Europe. Students and parents can join the vibrant parade, dance to the infectious rhythms of Calypso and Soca music, and indulge in delicious Caribbean cuisine. The Notting Hill Carnival is an experience that will leave lasting memories for the whole family.

Another traditional festival that should not be missed is the Lord Mayor's Show, held every November. This grand event dates back to the 12th century and celebrates the inauguration of the new Lord Mayor of the City of London. Students and parents can witness the spectacular procession of the Lord Mayor's golden coach, accompanied by marching bands, colorful floats, and a stunning display of fireworks. The Lord Mayor's Show is a true spectacle that showcases the rich history and pageantry of London.

For those interested in Christmas traditions, the Winter Wonderland festival in Hyde Park is a must-visit. This magical event transforms the Park into a winter wonderland, complete with ice skating rinks, festive markets, and a giant Ferris wheel. Students and parents can enjoy a day of fun-filled activities, including fairground rides, live entertainment, and even a chance to meet Santa Claus himself. The Winter Wonderland festival is the perfect way to get into the holiday spirit and create cherished family memories.

London's traditional festivals are not just about entertainment; they also provide valuable insights into the city's history and cultural heritage. By participating in these festivals, students and parents can gain a deeper appreciation for London's diverse traditions and its role as a melting pot of cultures.

In conclusion, London's traditional festivals offer a unique opportunity for students and parents to experience the city's rich culture and history. From the vibrant Notting Hill Carnival to the grand Lord Mayor's Show and the enchanting Winter Wonderland festival, there is something for everyone to enjoy. These festivals provide an immersive experience that will leave a lasting impression on the whole family, making London living truly unforgettable.

Contemporary Cultural Festivals Showcasing Diversity

London is renowned for its vibrant and diverse art and cultural scene, and one of the best ways to experience this is through the city's contemporary cultural festivals. These festivals celebrate the rich diversity of London's population, showcasing a wide range of artistic expressions, traditions, and cultures from around the world. For students and parents looking to immerse themselves in the city's cultural offerings, these festivals provide a unique opportunity to learn and appreciate different art forms while also having a fun and enjoyable experience.

One such festival is the Notting Hill Carnival, held annually in August. This vibrant event celebrates Caribbean culture and is one of the largest street festivals in Europe. The carnival features colorful costumes, lively music, and delicious Caribbean food, creating a truly immersive experience for attendees. Students and parents can enjoy the parades, dance to the rhythms of steel bands, and explore the stalls selling traditional crafts and cuisine.

For those interested in exploring different cultures, the Southbank Centre's Festival of World Cultures is a must-visit. This festival brings together artists, musicians, and performers from all corners of the globe, offering a diverse program of events and activities. From traditional dance performances to contemporary art installations, this festival provides a unique insight into cultures from around the world. Students and parents can participate in workshops, attend talks, and enjoy live music performances, making it a perfect opportunity for cultural exchange and learning.

Another festival that showcases the diversity of London's cultural scene is the Africa Centre Summer Festival. Held in Trafalgar Square, this festival celebrates African heritage through music, dance, food, and art. Students and parents can experience the vibrant rhythms of African music, taste delicious African cuisine, and explore the stalls selling handmade crafts and clothing. The festival also features workshops and activities for children, making it a great family-friendly event.

These contemporary cultural festivals are just a glimpse into the rich and diverse arts and cultural scene in London. Whether you are a student or a parent, exploring these festivals will not only provide a fun and enjoyable experience but also broaden your horizons and deepen your appreciation for different cultures. With a calendar full of exciting events throughout the year, London truly is a city that celebrates diversity and offers something for everyone.

Seasonal Festivals: Winter Markets, Summer Shows, and More

London is a vibrant city that comes alive with a wide array of festivals and cultural events throughout the year. From winter markets to summer shows, there is always something exciting happening in the city. In this subchapter, we will explore some of the seasonal festivals that take place in London, catering to both families and art enthusiasts.

Winter markets are a highlight of the festive season in London. The city transforms into a winter wonderland with charming markets popping up all over town. From the iconic Winter Wonderland in Hyde Park to the Southbank Centre Winter Market, these markets offer a plethora of stalls selling everything from unique gifts to delicious food and drinks. Families can enjoy ice skating fairground rides and even meet Santa Claus himself.

As summer approaches, London's cultural scene bursts into life with a range of shows and festivals. The West End takes center stage with its world-renowned theaters showcasing fantastic musicals and plays. From the classics like The Lion King to new productions, there is something for everyone to enjoy. Students with a keen interest in the arts will be delighted by the diverse range of performances on offer.

Music lovers are in for a treat during the summer months, with numerous music festivals taking place across the city. From the iconic British Summer Time in Hyde Park to smaller, more intimate events, there is a festival to suit every taste. Students and parents can groove to the sounds of their favorite artists, discover new talent, and soak up the vibrant atmosphere of the London music scene.

Beyond the winter markets and summer shows, London also hosts a variety of cultural events throughout the year. The city's museums and galleries regularly hold special exhibitions, allowing visitors to immerse themselves in art and history. From contemporary art at the Tate Modern to the British Museum's extensive collection, there is no shortage of cultural experiences to be had.

In conclusion, London offers an abundance of seasonal festivals and cultural events that cater to both families and art enthusiasts. Whether it's exploring winter markets, enjoying summer shows, or immersing oneself in the city's vibrant cultural scene, there is always something exciting happening in London. So, whether you're a student or a parent, make sure to check out these seasonal festivals and create unforgettable memories in this incredible city.

Chapter 6: Embracing Cultural Events in London

Literary Festivals: A Haven for Bookworms

For students and parents who have a love for literature, London is a city rich in literary festivals that offer a haven for bookworms. These festivals celebrate the written word, bringing together renowned authors, emerging writers, and avid readers in a vibrant and engaging environment. In this subchapter, we will explore the exciting world of literary festivals in London, their significance, and the opportunities they provide for both education and entertainment.

London's literary festivals offer a unique platform for students and parents to immerse themselves in the world of books, fostering a love for reading and nurturing intellectual curiosity. These events are not only educational but also enjoyable, providing a wonderful opportunity to engage with like-minded individuals who share a passion for literature.

One of the most prominent literary festivals in London is the London Literature Festival, held annually at the Southbank Centre. This festival features a diverse range of events, including author talks, panel discussions, book signings, and workshops. It showcases both established and emerging literary voices, giving students and parents a chance to hear from their favorite authors and discover new talents.

Another notable festival is the Chiswick Book Festival, a community-led event that celebrates literature and raises funds for local charities. This festival offers a range of activities suitable fo children, such as storytelling sessions, creative workshops, and interactive performances. It provides a family-friendly atmosphere where young readers can explore their imagination and develop a lifelong love for books.

Literary festivals also present opportunities for students to enhance their educational experience. The London Book Fair, for instance, focuses on the publishing industry and offers insights into the world of books, from writing and editing to marketing and distribution. Students interested in pursuing careers in writing, journalism, or publishing can gain valuable knowledge and network with industry professionals.

Moreover, these festivals often feature book markets and stalls, allowing attendees to explore a vast collection of books, both new releases and timeless classics. Students and parents can browse through the stalls, discover new authors, and expand their personal libraries with captivating reads.

In conclusion, London's literary festivals provide a haven for bookworms, offering a range of educational and entertaining opportunities for students and parents. These events celebrate literature, bringing together renowned authors, emerging writers, and passionate readers. Whether attending author talks, participating in workshops, or exploring book markets, these festivals offer a unique environment to foster a love for reading, inspire creativity, and create lasting memories.

Film Festivals: Showcasing the Best of Cinema

Film festivals are an integral part of the vibrant arts and culture scene in London, and they offer a unique platform to showcase the best of cinema from around the world. These festivals bring together filmmakers, industry professionals, and movie enthusiasts to celebrate the art of storytelling through film.

London is home to numerous film festivals that cater to a diverse range of genres and interests. From international blockbusters to independent productions, there is something for everyone. These festivals not only provide a platform for established filmmakers but also serve as a launching pad for upcoming talent.

One of the most prestigious film festivals in London is the BFI London Film Festival. Held annually in October, it showcases a wide range of films, from mainstream hits to thought-provoking documentaries and experimental works. The festival attracts renowned directors, actors, and industry professionals, making it a must-visit event for cinema lovers.

For families looking to introduce their children to the world of cinema, the Into Film Festival is a great option. This festival focuses on films suitable for young audiences and offers screenings, workshops, and Q&A sessions with filmmakers. It provides a fun and educational experience, allowing children to explore different aspects of filmmaking and storytelling.

In addition to these mainstream film festivals, London also hosts niche festivals that cater to specific genres or cultural backgrounds. The BFI Flare: London LGBTQ+ Film Festival celebrates the diversity and creativity of LGBTQ+ storytelling. The Raindance Film Festival showcases independent films from around the world, giving a platform to emerging filmmakers.

Attending a film festival in London is not only a chance to watch incredible films but also an opportunity to engage with the filmmaking community. Q&A sessions, panel discussions, and workshops provide a unique insight into the creative process and allow attendees to interact with industry professionals.

Whether you are a student looking to explore the world of cinema or a parent seeking family-friendly cultural experiences, London's film festivals offer a plethora of options. From the glitz and glamour of the red carpet to thought-provoking documentaries, these festivals create a vibrant atmosphere that celebrates the art of filmmaking. So, mark your calendars and immerse yourself in the magic of cinema at one of London's many film festivals.

Performance Art and Dance Events: Pushing Boundaries

In the vibrant city of London, the arts and culture scene is constantly evolving and pushing boundaries. This subchapter explores the exciting world of performance art and dance events, where creativity knows no limits and innovation takes center stage. Whether you are a student or a parent, London offers a plethora of opportunities to experience these dynamic and thought-provoking forms of expression.

Performance art, often considered a fusion of visual art and theater, challenges traditional notions of what constitutes art. It blurs the lines between artist and spectator, inviting the audience to actively engage with the experience. London is a hotbed for performance art, with galleries and alternative spaces hosting a range of groundbreaking and experimental performances. From immersive installations to interactive performances, you will find yourself transported into a world of imagination and creativity.

Dance events in London are equally awe-inspiring, offering a diverse range of styles and performances. From classical ballet to contemporary dance, there is something for everyone to enjoy. The city boasts world-renowned dance companies such as the Royal Ballet and Sadler's Wells, where you can witness breathtaking performances by some of the finest dancers in the world. Additionally, London is home to numerous dance festivals and showcases that celebrate the richness and diversity of this art form.

What sets London's performance art and dance events apart is their ability to push boundaries and challenge societal norms. Artists and choreographers constantly strive to break new ground, exploring themes of identity, politics, and social change. These thought-provoking performances not only entertain but also provide a platform for critical dialogue and reflection.

For families, there are plenty of family-friendly performance art and dance events in London.

Many theaters and galleries offer special programs and workshops designed to engage children and introduce them to the world of art and dance. From interactive exhibitions to child-friendly ballet performances, these events provide a unique opportunity for children to explore their creativity and develop an appreciation for the arts.

So, whether you are a student eager to explore the avant-garde or a parent looking for a cultural experience to share with your children, London's performance art and dance events are sure to captivate and inspire. Step outside your comfort zone and embrace the world of creativity that awaits you in this vibrant city. Get ready to have your boundaries pushed and your imagination ignited as you delve into the captivating world of performance art and dance in London.

Chapter 7: London Living for Families

Finding Family-Friendly Neighborhoods in London

London is a vibrant and diverse city that offers a wealth of opportunities for families. With its rich history, world-class museums, and stunning parks, there is no shortage of things to see and do. However, when it comes to finding the perfect neighborhood for your family, it's important to consider a few key factors. In this subchapter, we will explore the best family- friendly neighborhoods in London, along with the schools, parks, and activities that make them ideal for children.

One of the top family-friendly neighborhoods in London is Richmond. Located in southwest London, Richmond offers a mix of beautiful green spaces, excellent schools, and a strong sense of community. The area is home to Richmond Park, which is the largest royal Park in London and provides endless opportunities for outdoor activities such as cycling, picnicking, and wildlife spotting. Additionally, Richmond boasts a number of outstanding schools, both state and private, making it a popular choice for families.

Another great neighborhood for families is Greenwich. Situated on the banks of the River Thames, Greenwich is known for its historical significance and stunning architecture. The area is home to the Royal Observatory, where families can explore the wonders of the universe, as well as the National Maritime Museum, which offers interactive exhibits for children of all ages. With its abundance of green spaces and family-friendly amenities, Greenwich is a fantastic choice for families looking to immerse themselves in London's rich history and culture.

For families seeking a more urban vibe, Islington is an excellent choice. This trendy neighborhood is home to a number of world-class theaters, including the Almeida Theatre and the Sadler's Wells Theatre, both of which offer family-friendly performances and workshops. Islington also boasts a range of outstanding schools, as well as numerous parks and playgrounds, making it a great option for families who want to combine city living with a strong sense of community.

In conclusion, finding a family-friendly neighborhood in London is all about considering your family's needs and interests. Whether you prefer the green spaces and sense of community in Richmond, the historical significance of Greenwich, or the urban vibe of Islington, there is a neighborhood in London that will suit your family's lifestyle. By exploring the schools, parks, and activities available in each area, you can make an informed decision that will ensure your family's happiness and well-being in this exciting city.

Nurturing Education: Schools and Educational Institutions

In the bustling city of London, education takes center stage. With a rich cultural heritage and a vibrant arts scene, the city offers a plethora of opportunities for students to not only excel academically but also explore their artistic and creative talents. This subchapter aims to guide students and parents through the educational landscape of London, highlighting the various schools and educational institutions that foster a love for learning, arts, and culture.

London is home to a wide range of educational options catering to diverse interests and learning styles. From traditional public and private schools to specialized institutions, there is something for every student. Families looking for family-friendly neighborhoods, schools, parks, and activities suitable for children in London will find this section particularly helpful.

The chapter starts by exploring the top-ranked primary and secondary schools in the city. These institutions provide a strong foundation for students, combining rigorous academics with a focus on arts and culture. We delve into their unique teaching methods, extracurricular offerings, and success stories of notable alumni.

For those seeking alternative educational paths, London offers a plethora of specialized institutions. From performing arts schools to creative writing programs, students can hone their artistic talents while receiving a quality education. We highlight the renowned institutions that have produced some of the brightest stars in the arts and cultural scene.

Furthermore, this subchapter also provides insights into the various scholarships and grants available to students pursuing education in the arts and culture sector. London Living for Arts and Culture niche readers will find this section particularly valuable, as it provides information on how to access funding for artistic pursuits, whether it be attending a prestigious theater school or participating in a music festival.

Lastly, we explore the role of educational institutions in promoting cultural events and festivals in the city. Many schools collaborate with local galleries, theaters, and music venues to provide students with hands-on experiences and exposure to the arts. We highlight some of the most exciting collaborations and events happening in London, giving students and parents a glimpse into the vibrant cultural landscape of the city.

In conclusion, this subchapter aims to equip students and parents with the necessary information to navigate the educational landscape of London. Whether you are looking for a top- ranked school, a specialized institution, or funding for artistic pursuits, this chapter has you covered. London's commitment to nurturing education, arts, and culture ensures that students have access to a world-class education while immersing themselves in the vibrant artistic scene of the city.

Exploring Parks and Outdoor Spaces for Children

In this subchapter, we will delve into the vibrant world of parks and outdoor spaces that London has to offer for children. London is not just about its iconic landmarks and bustling city life; it also boasts a wide array of green spaces that provide endless opportunities for children to play, learn, and connect with nature. Whether you are a student or a parent, this chapter is designed to help you discover the best parks and outdoor spaces for children in the city.

London is renowned for its beautiful and well-maintained parks, which are not only perfect for picnics and leisurely strolls but also offer a host of activities specifically tailored for children. From the sprawling Hyde Park with its famous Serpentine Lake to the enchanting wonders of Regent's Park, there is something for everyone. These parks are equipped with playgrounds, sports facilities, and even wildlife encounters, making them ideal destinations for family outings.

For those seeking a more educational and interactive experience, London is home to several nature reserves and ecological centers. The London Wetland Centre, for instance, provides an immersive experience where children can get up close with a variety of bird species and learn about wetland habitats. Kew Gardens offers a similar experience with its stunning landscapes, conservatories, and educational exhibits.

Additionally, London has a multitude of adventure playgrounds that are sure to captivate the young ones. The Diana Princess of Wales Memorial Playground in Kensington Gardens, inspired by the story of Peter Pan, is a must-visit destination that encourages imaginative play. Meanwhile, Coram's Fields in Bloomsbury offers a unique space exclusively for children, complete with a city farm and sports facilities.

To enhance your exploration, consider joining organized activities and events happening in these parks. Many parks host seasonal festivals, outdoor cinemas, and even theater performances, providing an excellent opportunity for children to engage with the arts and culture. Keep an eye on the events calendar to make the most of your visit.

In conclusion, London's parks and outdoor spaces offer a diverse range of activities and experiences for children. Whether you are looking for a place to relax and enjoy nature or seeking interactive and educational encounters, London has it all. So grab your picnic blanket, put on your walking shoes, and embark on a journey of exploration in the city's beautiful parks and green spaces.

Engaging Activities Suitable for Children in London

London is a vibrant city that offers a plethora of engaging activities suitable for children. Whether you are a student or a parent, there is no shortage of exciting and educational opportunities for young ones to explore in this cultural hub. In this subchapter, we will delve into some of the best activities that will keep children entertained and enriched in London.

Museums are a fantastic way to spark a child's curiosity and love for learning. The city is home to world-renowned museums, such as the Natural History Museum and the Science Museum, which offer interactive exhibits and workshops designed specifically for children. From dinosaur fossils to space exploration, these museums provide an immersive and educational experience that is both entertaining and informative.

For those who have a passion for the arts, London's theater scene is a must-visit. The West End is famous for its dazzling array of musicals, plays, and performances suitable for all ages. Shows like ""The Lion King" and "Matilda" captivate young audiences with their enchanting storytelling and mesmerizing performances. Additionally, many theaters offer backstage tours and workshops, allowing children to get a behind-the-scenes glimpse into the world of theater.

Music lovers will also find plenty of venues and events to indulge in their passion. The Royal Albert Hall hosts family-friendly concerts throughout the year, featuring orchestras and performers from around the world. The London Symphony Orchestra also offers concerts tailored specifically for young listeners, introducing them to the magical world of classical music.

London's parks and green spaces provide the perfect setting for outdoor activities and family fun. Hyde Park, Regent's Park, and Richmond Park are just a few of the many beautiful parks scattered throughout the city. These green oases offer playgrounds, picnic areas, and even opportunities for boating and cycling, providing a welcome escape from the bustling city streets.

Lastly, festivals and cultural events are a highlight of London's vibrant arts and culture scene. The city hosts numerous family-friendly festivals throughout the year, celebrating music, art, theater, and more. The Mayor's Thames Festival, the Notting Hill Carnival, and the Winter Wonderland in Hyde Park are just a few examples of the exciting events that children can enjoy.

In conclusion, London is a treasure trove of engaging activities suitable for children. From museums and theaters to parks and festivals, there is something to captivate and inspire every young mind. Whether you are a student or a parent, London provides endless opportunities for families to embrace the city's rich arts and culture scene while creating lasting memories.

Chapter 8: Insider Tips for London Living

Navigating Public Transportation in the City

London is a vibrant and bustling city with a rich cultural scene that offers a plethora of art galleries, theaters, music venues, festivals, and cultural events. For students and parents looking to immerse themselves in the arts and culture of this city, it is essential to understand how to navigate its extensive public transportation system.

London's public transportation network is renowned for its efficiency and connectivity. The most commonly used modes of transportation include the iconic red double-decker buses, the Underground, and the Overground trains. These options provide easy access to all corners of the city, making it convenient for students and parents to explore the various cultural offerings.

The Underground, commonly known as the Tube, is the backbone of London's transportation system. With its extensive network of lines and stations, it is the quickest way to travel around the city. Each line is color-coded, and stations are well-signposted, making it relatively easy for newcomers to find their way. Students and parents should consider getting an Oyster card, a rechargeable smartcard that offers discounted fares and can be used on all modes of public transport.

In addition to the Tube, buses are a popular mode of transportation in London. The red double-decker buses are not only an iconic sight but also a convenient way to travel. They operate on an extensive network of routes, covering areas that may not be easily accessible by the Underground. Students and parents can use their Oyster cards or contactless payment methods to pay for their bus journeys.

For those looking to venture beyond the city center, the Overground trains provide excellent connectivity to the outskirts of London. These trains offer a comfortable and reliable mode of transportation, with regular services to popular cultural destinations such as Greenwich and Richmond.

Navigating public transportation in London may seem daunting at first, but with a little bit of planning and familiarity, it can quickly become second nature. Students and parents should take advantage of the available resources, such as online journey planners and smartphone apps, to map their routes and check for any disruptions or delays.

By mastering the art of navigating public transportation in London, students and parents can unlock the city's vibrant arts and cultural scene. From art galleries and theaters to music venues and festivals, there is no shortage of exciting events and activities to explore. So hop on a bus or dive into the Underground, and let London's cultural wonders unfold before your eyes.

Budget-Friendly Options for Arts and Cultural Experiences

London is a city renowned for its rich arts and cultural scene, offering a plethora of galleries, theaters, music venues, festivals, and cultural events. However, exploring these attractions can often come with a hefty price tag. For students and parents looking to experience the best of London's arts and culture without breaking the bank, we have compiled a list of budget-friendly options that will delight both children and adults alike.

Art Galleries:

London is home to some of the world's most prestigious art galleries, including the Tate Modern, the National Gallery, and the Victoria and Albert Museum. While these institutions often have entrance fees for special exhibitions, they also offer free access to their permanent collections. Take advantage of this opportunity to introduce your children to iconic works of art without spending a penny.

Theaters and Music Venues:

If you and your family are theater enthusiasts, London's West End is a must-visit destination. However, ticket prices for popular shows can be steep. Instead, consider exploring the city's vibrant fringe theater scene, where you can catch innovative performances at a fraction of the cost. Additionally, keep an eye out for discounted matinee performances or last-minute tickets available through theater websites and apps.

Festivals and Cultural Events:

London is a city that loves to celebrate, and throughout the year, it hosts a multitude of festivals and cultural events. From the Notting Hill Carnival to the Mayor's Thames Festival, these events offer a fantastic opportunity to immerse yourself in London's diverse culture. Many of these festivals are free to attend, providing an incredible experience for the whole family.

Alternative Cultural Experiences:

Beyond the traditional galleries and theaters, London offers a range of alternative cultural experiences that won't strain your budget. Visit independent art spaces such as the Whitechapel Gallery or Camden Arts Centre, which often host free exhibitions and events. Explore street art in neighborhoods like Shoreditch or Brixton, where you can witness vibrant murals and graffiti without spending a penny.

In conclusion, London's arts and cultural scene is accessible to students and parents on a budget. By taking advantage of free museum collections, exploring fringe theaters, attending festivals, and seeking out alternative cultural experiences, you can create unforgettable memories without emptying your wallet. So, grab your Oyster card and embark on a budget-friendly journey through London's vibrant arts and cultural landscape.

Making the Most of London's Free Attractions

In a city known for its vibrant arts and culture scene, London offers an array of free attractions that are perfect for students and parents looking to explore the city without breaking the bank. Whether you are a family looking for family-friendly activities or an art and culture enthusiast, London has something for everyone. This subchapter will guide you through some of the best free attractions in the city, ensuring you make the most of your time in London.

For families, London Living for Families emphasizes family-friendly neighborhoods, schools, parks, and activities suitable for children. One of the top recommendations is the Natural History Museum, a treasure trove of wonders that will captivate children and adults alike... Explore the dinosaur exhibit, marvel at the impressive blue whale skeleton, and discover the vast collection of minerals and fossils. The Science Museum is another must-visit for families, where interactive exhibits and hands-on experiments foster a love for science and technology.

London Living for Arts and Culture focuses on art galleries, theaters, music venues, festivals, and cultural events happening in London. One of the highlights for art enthusiasts is the Tate Modern, which houses an extensive collection of contemporary art. From iconic works by Picasso and Warhol to thought-provoking installations, the Tate Modern offers a unique artistic experience. For theater lovers, the National Theatre offers free outdoor performances during the summer months, allowing you to enjoy world-class productions against the backdrop of the stunning River Thames.

In addition to these renowned attractions, London also boasts numerous parks and green spaces where families can unwind and enjoy the city's natural beauty. Hyde Park, Regent's Park, and Richmond Park are just a few examples of London's stunning parks, perfect for picnics, leisurely walks, and even spotting wildlife.

To make the most of London's free attractions, it is essential to plan your visit in advance. Many museums and galleries offer free entry, but some may require pre-booking or have specific visiting hours. By researching and planning ahead, you can ensure a seamless and enjoyable experience.

London Living for Arts and Culture: Exploring Galleries, Theaters, Music Venues, Festivals, and Cultural Events in the City provides a comprehensive guide to London's free attractions, catering to the interests of both students and parents. By immersing yourself in the city's rich cultural offerings, you can create lasting memories and discover the true essence of London.

Safety, Security, and Practical Considerations

When it comes to living in any city, safety and security are always top priorities. As students and parents considering a move to London, it is essential to be aware of the measures in place to ensure your well-being. This subchapter will provide you with valuable information on safety, security, and practical considerations to help you make informed decisions and enjoy a worry-free experience while exploring the vibrant arts and culture scene of this magnificent city.

London has a reputation as one of the safest cities in the world, but it is still important to exercise caution and be aware of your surroundings. The city has an extensive network of police stations and CCTV cameras, ensuring that assistance is readily available if needed. Additionally, the presence of security personnel in popular areas such as galleries, theaters, and music venues contributes to a sense of security.

When it comes to practical considerations, transportation is a key factor. London boasts a comprehensive public transportation system, including buses, the iconic Underground, and trains, allowing easy access to various cultural events and venues. It is advisable to familiarize yourself with the different routes and timetables to make the most of your time in the city.

Another crucial aspect to consider is accommodation. London offers a wide variety of family-friendly neighborhoods, ensuring that you find the perfect place to call home. From leafy suburbs with excellent schools and parks to vibrant areas with a bustling arts and culture scene, there is something for everyone. Researching the different neighborhoods and their amenities will help you make an informed decision that suits your family's needs and preferences.

Additionally, it is worth exploring the numerous family-friendly activities and attractions that London has to offer. From interactive museums and beautiful parks to child-friendly theaters and festivals, there is no shortage of entertainment suitable for children. These venues often have safety measures in place, such as designated play areas and trained staff, ensuring a safe and enjoyable experience for the whole family.

In conclusion, London provides a safe and secure environment for students and families alike to explore its rich arts and culture scene. By being aware of practical considerations such as transportation and accommodation, as well as the family-friendly activities available, you can fully immerse yourself in the vibrant cultural events and make the most of your time in this enchanting city.

Chapter 9: Conclusion: Embracing London's Arts, Culture, and Family-Friendly Living

Reflecting on the Richness of London's Arts and Culture Scene

London, a city steeped in history and known for its vibrant arts and culture scene, offers a wealth of opportunities for students and parents alike to immerse themselves in a world of creativity and inspiration. From world-class art galleries to iconic theaters, music venues, festivals, and cultural events, London truly is a haven for arts and culture enthusiasts.

Art Galleries:

London is home to some of the most renowned art galleries in the world, such as the Tate Modern, the National Gallery, and the Victoria and Albert Museum. These institutions house a vast collection of masterpieces from various periods, allowing students and parents to explore the rich tapestry of artistic expression throughout history. Whether it's admiring classical paintings, contemporary installations, or thought-provoking sculptures, these galleries offer a unique and enlightening experience for art lovers of all ages.

Theaters:

For those with a passion for the performing arts, London's West End is a must-visit. With its world-famous theaters showcasing a wide array of productions, including musicals, plays, and dance performances, there is something to captivate every audience member. From long-running favorites like "The Lion King" and "Les Misérables" to exciting new productions, the West End is a stage where dreams come to life, leaving a lasting impression on students and parents alike.

Music Venues and Festivals:

London's music scene is as diverse as its population, offering a platform for both established and emerging artists. From intimate jazz clubs to iconic venues like the Royal Albert Hall, there are endless opportunities to immerse oneself in a variety of musical genres. Additionally, the city hosts numerous music festivals throughout the year, such as the British Summer Time Festival in Hyde Park and the Notting Hill Carnival, where students and parents can experience the joy of live music and celebration.

Cultural Events:

London's cultural calendar is packed with exciting events that celebrate the city's multicultural heritage. From the colorful Chinese New Year festivities in Chinatown to the vibrant Diwali celebrations in Trafalgar Square, these events provide a window into different cultures and traditions. Students and parents can partake in parades, performances, and culinary delights, fostering a deeper understanding and appreciation of London's diverse community.

In conclusion, London's arts and culture scene offers a treasure trove of experiences for students and parents seeking to enrich their lives through the exploration of galleries, theaters, music venues, festivals, and cultural events. Whether it's immersing oneself in the beauty of art, being transported by the magic of theater, or embracing the rhythm of live music, London truly is a city that nurtures the soul and ignites the imagination.

Creating Lasting Memories as a Family in the City

As students and parents living in the vibrant city of London, it's essential to make the most of your time together as a family and create lasting memories. Despite the bustling urban environment, there are numerous family-friendly activities, neighborhoods, and cultural events that cater to both children and adults. In this subchapter, we will explore how you can make the most of your time as a family, emphasizing family-friendly neighborhoods, schools, parks, and activities suitable for children in London while also focusing on the city's art galleries, theaters, music venues, festivals, and cultural events.

London is known for its family-friendly neighborhoods, where you can find excellent schools and a range of activities suitable for children. Areas like Richmond, Greenwich, and Hampstead offer a perfect blend of educational institutions, parks, and recreational facilities that cater to families. These neighborhoods provide a safe and nurturing environment for children to grow and thrive.

When it comes to parks and green spaces, London has an abundance of options. From the iconic Hyde Park and Regent's Park to hidden gems like Battersea Park and Kew Gardens, there is no shortage of places to spend quality time with your family. These parks often host family-oriented events and festivals, providing an opportunity to immerse yourselves in the city's culture while enjoying outdoor activities.

London is also a hub for arts and culture, offering a plethora of opportunities for families to engage in creative pursuits. The city is home to world-renowned art galleries such as the Tate Modern and the National Gallery, which regularly organize family-friendly exhibitions and workshops. The West End boasts an array of theaters showcasing captivating plays and musicals suitable for all ages. Additionally, London hosts numerous music festivals and cultural events throughout the year, bringing together people from diverse backgrounds to celebrate the city's rich heritage.

By actively participating in these cultural events and exploring the family-friendly neighborhoods, schools, parks, and activities that London has to offer, you can create lasting memories with your loved ones. Whether it's attending a play together, exploring an art exhibition, or simply enjoying a picnic in one of the city's parks, there are endless opportunities to bond as a family while immersing yourselves in the vibrant culture of London.

In the following chapters, we will delve deeper into specific neighborhoods, schools, parks, and cultural events that cater to families, ensuring you make the most of your time together and create unforgettable memories in this dynamic city.

Loving my travel adventures as Professor of US EU law!

19.03.24

Helsinki South Harbour ⚓ 24.03.2024

Kapellbrücke Luzern.

Luzern am See.

Spring in Vienna 🌸☀🌸

©🌿 Alexandra Lhotak

Amazing beautiful

Villefranche-sur-Mer, France.

Prague, Czech Republic

About the Author

My first book: "A Joyful Professor's Global Journey" was a heartfelt thank you to all my teachers in life and especially my parents! This book is a thank you to my British wife first during my military and incredible law school and attorney growth years, and then my Dutch wife who was the beautiful mom of my darling daughters and was also very supportive while I earned all my other degrees as follows:

I earned my LL M, in taxation at Golden Gate University after having served in the US military - NATO -deployed to Germany, as an Army Captain and Company Commander- Then after my tour of duty, moving on to work as a Bank Officer for United California bank, then managing the City Treasurer's office at the City Of Huntington Beach, Ca - While attending Law School at night- and eventually becoming a Deputy City Attorney, after becoming an Attorney in California- where I led and participated in the largest municipal bankruptcy case in the history of the United States- Winning a large sum of money on behalf of my client, the City Of Huntington Beach, and other public entities similarly situated.

Then, I decided to continue my education with other working adults at Golden Gate, Pepperdine, and Hastings University. I was so blessed to have a Wonderful wife from the Netherlands, and the study of International Taxation was important. I eventually went on to live in the U.K., Switzerland, and The Netherlands, while teaching globally as a university professor -courses in International Law and Taxation for Webster University, in London, then Geneva, and then, the Hague " the Legal Capital of the World "in the Netherlands.

I then created a travel study Undergraduate and Graduate course, called "Comparative US / EU Law" while in Europe, and took students from London to Brussels, Brugge, Amsterdam, and then to Paris. That was such a success that I then created another course and we traveled from Venice to Nice, Monte Carlo to Florence and then Rome, and then back to Venice.

There is a saying that "an expert is defined as anyone from out of town" and so when I was teaching all over Europe I received the warmest welcomes and attended many events that were designed solely for ambassadors from other countries, especially in the city where most Ambassadors had homes, Wassenaar, Netherlands, and I was invited to meet up with some very, very special people like the Ambassador from India, who invited me to his home to meet other ambassadors from all over the world.

Some of the Ambassadors were kind enough to accept my invitation to give presentations at the World Trade Center in Amsterdam - for the organization I developed in The Netherlands - "The Center for the Advancement of Women and Diversity in Business"(see videos on Youtube") - my two lovely daughters even attended and ultimately became teachers as well due to this wonderful exposure and of course a very supportive Dutch Mom.

They attended school at Midhurst Elementary, while I was teaching in London, and, at one point we even watched Then, Prince Charles and his sons play polo at the polo grounds, Cowdray Park, "Cowdray Park Polo Club"

Sports club in Easebourne, England - "directly across the street from their school in Midhurst the United Kingdom when I was teaching in London, consequently I've always been thankful and very grateful for my teachers and professors, my military instructors and other professionals all through life, as well as my parents who purchased an Encyclopedia Britannica at a time when we could scarcely afford food - and taught us the true value and life meaning of books.

My father said to me, "Son, get an education they can never take it away from you." Clearly he was correct . The fact that my classes first in London, catered to working adults was a perfect match for me, and those of my future students - in Switzerland, and The Netherlands, similarly situated - and inspired all who participated, especially me!

One of my classes was in downtown Los Angeles very close to the corner where I used to shine shoes and sell newspapers, as a poor boy - due to my dad being a brave wounded US soldier.

I now live and a homeowner in one of the wealthiest parts of California, Newport Beach - where my neighbors are TV and Rock Stars and millionaires- and where my Law clients parked their yachts in front of my waterfront Law Office at Lido Marina Village.

I'm now writing a third book about my next Global Adventure with thanks to all who inspired me, especially all teachers in life, including my lovely family, fellow students, and professors alike- Much more to come later, when it is published in the next 30-69 days.